# 100

## THINGS TO DO IN SAN FRANCISCO BEFORE YOU DIE

# 100

## THINGS TO DO IN SAN FRANCISCO BEFORE YOU

# DIE

**· · · · · · · · · · · · · · · · · · · · · · · · · ·**

## EVE BATEY AND PATRICIA CORRIGAN

REEDY PRESS
St. Louis, Missouri

Reedy Press
PO Box 5131
St. Louis, MO 63139, USA
www.reedypress.com

Library of Congress Control Number: 2014946118

ISBN: 9781935806813

Design by Jill Halpin
Photos by Patricia Corrigan

Printed in the United States of America
14 15 16 17 18    5 4 3 2 1

Please note that websites, phone numbers, addresses, and company names are subject to change or cancellation. We did our best to relay the most accurate information available, but due to circumstances beyond our control, please do not hold us liable for misinformation. When exploring new destinations, please do your homework before you go.

# CONTENTS

• • • • • • • • • • • • • • • • • • • • • • •

# DEDICATION

We dedicate this book to you, in the hope that it will help you find far more than 100 things to do in San Francisco. Also, we are grateful to those who welcomed us when we arrived, guided us to many amazing places, and encouraged us to find others on our own.

# PREFACE

In *100 Things to Do in San Francisco Before You Die*, we talk top attractions, but we also make it easy for you to find a Mission-style burrito, rent a bike in Golden Gate Park, get tipsy on an alcoholic malt, buy designer clothing, join a sea chantey sing-along, shop for tie-dye in Haight-Ashbury, and see the new Exploratorium with the kids. We invite you to experience yoga on a labyrinth, a RocketBoat ride on the Bay, a tasty tea leaf salad, or a ride on a historic streetcar.

We encourage you to walk across the Golden Gate Bridge, sample Dungeness crab in season, rock out at a free musical festival, catch a Giants game, share a community table at a neighborhood eatery, pay tribute to our literary heritage, and visit our museums, including large (the de Young), small (the Beat Museum), and on the water (Alcatraz Island).

In these pages, you'll learn how to get to know San Francisco by bus, boat, bike, or Segway, and where to sign up for a walking tour. We also point you toward urban hiking trails with an ocean view, introduce you to a giant Pacific octopus at the California Academy of Sciences, and urge you to relax in a redwood grove at the Botanical Garden.

Every visitor quickly learns that any smile offered will be warmly returned in this big little town—so come to San Francisco!

P.S. We admit our weather is confusing. It's chilly in the summer and warm in the fall, and temperatures may vary as much as twenty degrees depending on the neighborhood. Be prepared for our microclimates and the ever-changing weather: bring layers!

# AS OTHERS SEE US

San Francisco's past informs so much of what this amazing city is today. Here are thoughts expressed over the years that still hold true.

"You wouldn't think such a place as San Francisco could exist. The wonderful sunlight here, the hills, the great bridges, the Pacific at your shoes. Beautiful Chinatown. Every race in the world. The sardine fleets sailing out. The little cable cars whizzing down The City hills. . . . And all the people are open and friendly."
*—Dylan Thomas, poet and writer*

"I never meet anyone who doesn't love the place, Americans or others."
*—Doris Lessing, writer*

"San Francisco is one of the great cultural plateaus in the world. . . . one of the really urbane communities in the United States . . . one of the truly cosmopolitan places—and for many, many years, it has always had a warm welcome for human beings from all over the world."
*—Duke Ellington, jazz legend*

"San Francisco is 49 square miles surrounded by reality."
*—Paul Kantner, musician, cofounder of Jefferson Airplane*

• • • • • • • • • • • • • • • • • • • • • • •

"I like the fog that creeps over the whole city every night about five, and the warm protective feeling it gives. . . . and lights of San Francisco at night, the fog horn, the bay at dusk and the little flower stands where spring flowers appear before anywhere else in the country. . . . But, most of all, I like the view of the ocean from the Cliff House."

—*Irene Dunne, actor*

"If it were necessary to pay admission to get into San Francisco, I'd pay it and never leave."

—*William Saroyan, writer*

● ● ● ● ● ● ● ● ● ● ● ● ● ● ● ● ● ● ● ● ● ● ● ● ● ● ●

# 100

## THINGS TO DO IN
## SAN FRANCISCO
## BEFORE YOU
# DIE

# FOOD AND DRINK

# TRY A LITTLE TENDERLOIN
## AT GARIBALDI'S

If lamb soothes your soul and you seek an alternative to a basic rack or shank, Garibaldi's brings to the table a special treat: marinated lamb tenderloins. "Each bite is better than the last," raves a native San Franciscan who orders the same dish every time. The tenderloins are served with couscous, pistachios, currants, and green beans, all topped with a rich tarragon sauce.

A special occasion spot for more than twenty years, Garibaldi's offers a cozy back room for semi-private dining or "see and be seen" tables up front. Either way, it's all low lights, white tablecloths, and a cozy atmosphere. If you save room (and haven't blown the budget yet), Garibaldi's offers outstanding chocolate budino with espresso ice cream, salted caramel sauce, and pralines.

*347 Presidio Avenue in Presidio Heights*
*415-563-8841, hurleyhafen.com/garibaldi*

**Tip:** *If it's fish you fancy, consider Tadich Grill (240 California Street in the Financial District), the iconic seafood restaurant that opened during the gold rush as a coffee stand.*

# PICK A PIZZA, ANY PIZZA

Some ponder the perfect combination of toppings, some place the highest value on a piquant sauce (whether red, white, or green), and some pay particular attention to the crust—everybody's standards differ when it comes to the perfect pizza!

Good pizza is abundant in San Francisco and is available at upscale dining spots, neighborhood bistros, corner bars, and by the slice at many a carryout place. Just pick one—or let us help. Here are three favorite spots and their specialties.

**Ragazza** *(potato pizza with applewood-smoked bacon)*
*311 Divisadero Street in the Lower Haight*
*415-255-1133, ragazzasf.com*

**Pauline's Pizza** *(pesto pizza)*
*260 Valencia Street in the Mission*
*415-552-2050, paulinespizza.com*

**Little Star Pizza** *(Chicago-style, deep-dish pizza)*
*400 Valencia Street in the Mission*
*415-551-7827*
*or*
*846 Divisadero Street in the Western Addition*
*415-441-1118, littlestarpizza.com*

**Tip:** *PizzaHacker in Bernal Heights, which started as a street food cart, is getting great buzz for its top-shelf margherita pie.*

# ZIP OVER TO ZUNI
## FOR ROASTED CHICKEN

If you believe that the simpler the dish, the more sophisticated the flavors, then set your course for the upscale Zuni Café, where the succulent roasted chicken is legendary, and rightly so. A dish for two, the free-range bird is slow-roasted in a brick oven, so expect to wait an hour for it to cook. When you take your first bite of tender, juicy, perfectly seasoned chicken, you will know the wait was worth it. This specialty of the house is served with warm bread salad.

Part of the restaurant scene here since 1979, Zuni makes the most of its unusual wedge-shaped building, with sleek decor and appealing brickwork inside and plenty of windows. Sit upstairs or down, and feast on traditional regional French and Italian dishes, all made with fresh and sustainably harvested ingredients

*1658 Market Street near the Civic Center*
*415-552-2522, zunicafe.com*

# RALLY 'ROUND THE REUBEN
## AT MEMPHIS MINNIE'S

If you're in need of a Reuben and it's a Wednesday, you're in luck!

Head for Memphis Minnie's Barbecue Joint, where the daily special on Wednesday is mouth-watering, house-cured and smoked brisket paired with Swiss cheese, sauerkraut, and Russian dressing, all piled on grilled rye. Any other day, opt for the tasty pulled pork or spicy chicken sandwiches or tackle a plate of perfect slow-smoked rib tips.

Like so many good barbecue restaurants, this is a true joint—don't expect fancy decor. Do expect lots of ceramic tributes to the mighty pig and a sign that reads: "Be Nice or Leave." All the meat at Minnie's is cooked over heat and smoke from burning white oak logs, and all the barbecue sauces and desserts (including pecan pie) are homemade. Plus, if you're a fan of cornbread muffins, this is the place for you.

*576 Haight Street in the Lower Haight*
*415-864-7675, memphisminnies.com*

**Tip:** *Craving deli? Look to Wise Sons Jewish Delicatessen (in the Mission and downtown) and the new Rye Project (in SoMa).*

# APPEASE YOUR BACON FIXATION
## AT APERTO

Need a bacon fix that a basic BLT or a grilled cheese with bacon won't satisfy?

Meet pepati, a savory pasta dish served at Aperto, a cozy neighborhood restaurant. A most generous portion of pungent smoked bacon comes nestled among the tagliolini, garlic, arugula, jalapeño slices, and two types of Italian cheese, all presented in a rich roasted tomato sauce. This is a dish to devour and then dream about for days!

A homey trattoria with sunny yellow walls, Aperto changes the menu to match what's in season and always offers daily specials plus prix-fixe meals at lunch and dinner. Vegetarians will be delighted with a selection of meat-free pastas and risottos and everyone at your table will gobble up the grilled Italian cheeses served on country bread. Dolce, a warm chocolate soufflé, is a superb dessert.

*1434 18th Street in Potrero Hill*
*415-252-1625, apertosf.com*

# MAKE ROOM
## FOR A MISSION BURRITO

San Francisco's burritos are a special breed. Since the 1960s, we've been making them bigger than anywhere else in the world, and many of the best are found in the Mission District. This is by no means a comprehensive list!

**Taqueria La Cumbre** (apocryphally the birthplace of the Mission burrito)
515 Valencia Street, 415 863-8205, taquerialacumbre.com

**La Taqueria** (Their no-rice policy packs each burrito with flavor.)
2889 Mission Street
415-285-7117

**Taqueria Cancún** (a vegetarian fave)
2288 Mission Street, 415-252-9560
3211 Mission Street, 415-550-1414
1003 Market Street, 415-252-9560

**El Farolito Taqueria** (an after-a-long-night-at-the-bar classic)
2779 Mission Street, 415-824-7887
4817 Mission Street, 415-337-5500
2950 24th Street, 415-641-0758
elfarolitoinc.com

**Pancho Villa Taqueria** (Dubbed "the French Laundry of taquerias.")
3071 16th Street, 415-864-8840, sfpanchovilla.com

**Tip:** *If you ever run out of things to talk about with San Franciscans, ask us where to find the best burrito.
We'll handle the talking for the next couple hours.*

# CELEBRATE
## UPSCALE MEXICAN CUISINE AT NOPALITO

If you like your Mexican more upscale, we can deliver on that too. Nopalito represents the quintessential Mexican kitchen, with flavorful dishes prepared from local, organic, sustainably grown or produced food. Every meal here starts with a small bowl of fried garbanzo beans, and we bet you can't eat just one bowl. At lunch, our standard order is enchiladas de mole con pollo and at dinner we go for birria de res (beef stewed in ancho chiles) or pozole rojo. Of course you can always get a terrific margarita, but if you're off the sauce, try the almond horchata, a traditional Mexican drink.

Nopalito has earnest roots—two cooks at the iconic Nopa, where Mediterranean fare rules, used to prepare dishes from their childhoods for the staff meal. Nopa's owners were so impressed they opened Nopalito, which now has two locations, both on the small side. After the first bite, you'll forget all about that.

**Nopalito**
*306 Broderick Street in the Lower Haight*
*415-437-0303*
*or*
*1224 9th Avenue in the Inner Sunset*
*415-233-9966, nopalitosf.com*

**Tip:** *Other upscale Mexican options include Colibri Mexican Bistro (west of Union Square), Padrecito's (Cole Valley), and Tacolicious (in the Marina, the Mission, and North Beach).*

# SLURP UP A SNOWY PLOVER
## AT ANDYTOWN

Sure, you can get a great cup of coffee at Andytown Coffee Roasters, as they roast transparently sourced beans in-house and pour with well-deserved pride. But they have one truly unique offering that's worth a trip to the Outer Sunset: the Snowy Plover, which co-proprietor Lauren Crabbe tells us comprises "a double shot of espresso, brown sugar simple syrup, (and) bubbly water" poured over ice and topped with a dollop of freshly whipped cream. It's bitter and sweet, fatty and refreshing, all at once—a magical thing. Pair it with one of their in-house baked scones or corn muffins for a total sugar high, or with their authentically Irish griddle-baked soda bread for a heartier snack.

*3655 Lawton Street in the Outer Sunset*
*andytownsf.com*

**Tip:** *Have Fido in tow? There's a big jar of organic dog biscuits to the left of the door, free for the taking. Why should you be the only one who gets a treat?*

# SIP A COCKTAIL
## AT THE HISTORIC TWIN PEAKS TAVERN

One of only two watering holes in San Francisco to be honored with landmark status, the Twin Peaks Tavern's shining glass windows are the first thing many visitors see as they arrive in the Castro. Widely known as one of the first gay bars in the country with uncovered windows, the bar's then-owners said they didn't intend to make history when, in 1972, they remodeled to allow customers to look out and the world to look in.

These days, although nearly every gay bar is a place to see and be seen, Twin Peaks remains a popular place for customers of all ages and orientations. It's a true San Francisco institution.

*401 Castro Street in the Castro*
*415-864-9470, twinpeakstavern.com*

**Tip:** *Nab the window table in the partial mezzanine. It's truly the best people-watching seat in the Castro. Even better, the window is adjacent to the neighboring bakery, so you're basically breathing cookie air.*

# DOWN SOME DIM SUM

The first thing you need to know is that San Francisco's best dim sum is not in Chinatown. Yes, it's counterintuitive, but to get the city's best of this Far East treat, you'll need to travel far further west. Don't worry if you're new to the delights of dim sum, as San Francisco is a great place to start your love affair with these bite-sized sweet and savory delights.

### Ton Kiang
*(Best pick for those just dipping their toes in the dim sum pond.)*
*5821 Geary Boulevard in the Richmond District*
*415-387-8273, tonkiang.net*

### S&T Hong Kong Seafood Restaurant
*(Get the shrimp noodle roll; you won't regret it.)*
*2578 Noriega Street in the Outer Sunset, 415-665-8338*

### Shanghai Dumpling King
*(This is for folks who want the "real," sometimes gritty, dim sum experience. Not for the faint of heart!)*
*3319 Balboa Street in the Richmond District, 415-387-2088*

### Yank Sing
*(If you're looking for a fancy, luxe dim sum date, this is your place.)*
*101 Spear Street in the Financial District, 415-781-1111*
*or*
*49 Stevenson Street in the Financial District*
*415-541-4949, yanksing.com*

# TASTE A TEA LEAF SALAD

Some consider tea leaf salad to be the national dish of Burma, and the crowds that line up outside San Francisco's Burmese joints demonstrate a fervor you might not expect for a salad. Try this combination of fermented tea leaves, dried nuts, seeds, and a variety of vegetables all spritzed with lemon and tossed at the table, and you'll be hooked. San Francisco has a wealth of Burmese restaurant options.

**Here are our favorites.**

**Burma Superstar** *(Get ready for a long wait at dinner time. If you're in a hurry, try this place at lunch instead.)*
*309 Clement Street in the Richmond District*
*415-387-2147, burmasuperstar.com*

**Burmese Kitchen** *(A grittier experience than some, this place has serious Burmese street cred.)*
*452 Larkin Street in the Tenderloin*
*415-474-5569, burmesekitchen.com*

**Mandalay** *(If you order "wrong" they yell at you, but that's part of their charm.)*
*4348 California Street in the Richmond District*
*415-386-3895, mandalaysf.com*

**Pagan** *(Friendly service, no wait, and a second Thai menu make this a locals' fave.)*
*3199 Clement Street in the Richmond District*
*415-751-2598, pagansf.com*

# CHOMP ON SAN FRANCISCO'S BEST SANDWICH
## AT ROXIE'S

We're almost afraid to tell you about the sandwiches at Roxie Food Center, because if other locals discover that we let the cat out of the bag, we'll be in big trouble. But how can we keep their amazing selection of sandwiches to ourselves?

Every sandwich, be it meatball, crab, or veggie, is the same price: $5.99 for a junior, $7.99 for a regular, and $11.99 for a supreme. Even the junior is a monster, with your choice of high-quality bread packed with meat, cheese, and a wide variety of veggies. Want changes or substitutions? No problem. Their service is impeccable, and no matter what requests you throw at them, Roxie's staff gets it right and serves you with a smile.

Served hot or cold, a Roxie's sandwich is worth the trip many locals make every week.

*1901 San Jose Avenue in Mission Terrace*
*415-587-2345*

**Tip:** *Get a Roxie's sandwich, then cut across town to Ocean Beach and eat while you watch the surfers come in as the sun sets. Give your leftovers to the seagulls. You're living the California dream.*

# TAKE STREET FOOD TO THE NEXT LEVEL
## AT SOMA STREAT FOOD PARK

SoMa StrEat Food Park turns the food truck trend into a vocation, as vendors (they rotate daily) park for lunch and dinner at their SoMa locale to serve up a head-spinning mix of comfort food, edgy cuisine, and guilty pleasures. Think of it as a food court for the adventurous. There's something for everyone at this place, so just keep walking and you'll find it. A beer and wine vendor is also on hand, and there is plenty of room to sit and enjoy your discoveries.

*429 11th Street, South of Market*
*somastreatfoodpark.com*

# DO SOME EXPLORING
## AT MARCO POLO ITALIAN ICE CREAM

Legend has it that famous explorer Marco Polo smuggled ice cream from China to Italy, and that nexus of Asian and Italian aesthetics sure makes sense when you visit Marco Polo. Known for unusual flavors like Arcobaleno (pistachio chocolate vanilla), taro, and their famous durian, the ice cream is as smooth and creamy as gelato. The tart fruit flavors combined with the rich fattiness of the cream make Marco Polo's unlike any ice cream you've had before.

Don't worry, you don't have to have an unusual flavor—they have plenty of traditional flavors too. But given their habit of offering generously sized free samples to the undecided, you have no excuse not to take a chance on something new. Just remember to hit the ATM beforehand, because Marco Polo is cash only.

*1447 Taraval Street in the Sunset*
*415-731-2833*

# BINGE ON A 21-OUNCE GOURMET BURGER
## AT BILL'S PLACE

OK, if the giant fiftieth-anniversary burger at Bill's Place is too much meat, you can choose from assorted sizes of cheeseburgers or more than a dozen additional gourmet patties. Some of them are named for (and in some cases, designed by) celebrities, including Beverly Sills, the Letterman band, Al "Jazz Beaux" Collins, Paul Kantner, Carol Doda, and wordsmith Herb Caen. You can even get a kiwi burger à la New Zealand, with beets and pineapple on top.

This family-owned burger joint also offers fresh-cut fries, chicken dishes, assorted sandwiches, and breakfast items. Best of all, you can split a giant milk shake with a friend and still have some left in the frosty metal container. (The creamy Black and White combines chocolate ice cream with vanilla.) Eat outside by the Japanese garden or in the dining room, where Bill's displays an award naming it one of the Best American Restaurants in the U.S.

*2315 Clement Street in the Richmond District*
*415-221-5262, billsplace.qpg.com*

# DIG INTO
# THE DRY FRIED CHICKEN
## AT SAN TUNG

"Dry" and "chicken" seem like a bad match until you get a bite of San Tung's dry fried goodness. Battered and deep fried with garlic, ginger, and roasted red peppers, these wings are more than the sum of their parts. San Tung is a San Francisco cult classic, with the lines and waits to prove it.

Of course, the chicken's not the only thing to order at San Tung: check out their many seafood offerings for taste combinations you never believed possible. Vegetarians also have abundant options, including some mushroom dishes containing ingredients so exotic looking they seem straight out of *The Lord of the Rings*.

For an ideal experience, go at an off hour (they're open from 11 A.M. to 9:30 P.M. daily, every day but Wednesday), load up the lazy Susan at your table's center, and chow down.

*1031 Irving Street in the Inner Sunset*
*415-242-0828, santungrestaurant.com*

**Tip:** *San Tung's owners recently opened another restaurant next to their original. If the wait at #1 is too long, nab a seat at #2!*

# EAT FARM FRESH
## AT THE FERRY BUILDING MARKETPLACE

The managers of San Francisco's Ferry Building have worked tirelessly to make sure every vendor in their beautiful building offers an only-in-SF experience, turning down overtures from chain restaurants or vendors, and taste-testing offerings from every prospective tenant.

Though you can visit the food and beverage retailers and restaurants any day of the week, Saturday is the Marketplace's day to shine, with the city's best farmers market springing up in front of and behind the structure from 8 A.M. to 2 P.M. There's also a smaller market from 10 A.M. to 2 P.M. on Tuesdays and Thursdays featuring a wide variety of artisan street food.

The Ferry Building is also one of the most beautiful venues in the city, from its light-filled, airy interior, to the exterior just feet from San Francisco Bay. While there's ample seating inside most Ferry Building venues, locals know to grab a bench on the south side of the building. Sit, savor, and watch traffic go by on the Bay Bridge.

*The Embarcadero at the east end of Market Street*
*415-983-8030, ferrybuildingmarketplace.com*

# WORK ON A KELLER'S FARM
## AT THE ICE CREAM BAR SODA FOUNTAIN

This isn't kid's stuff: the Ice Cream Bar Soda Fountain's offerings include old-school classics like phosphates, lactarts, malts, and (for adults only) alcohol-infused "remedies." One of the standout dishes on a menu full of treats is the Keller's Farm, which is cornmeal shortbread, creme fraiche and morello cherry ice creams, cherry sauce, and rosemary syrup.

Not in the mood for sweets? From noon to 10 P.M. daily, they also run a traditional soda fountain–style lunch service, serving old-school classics with an upscale twist, like a tuna melt with fontina and organic greens, or a PBJ with house-made peanut butter and organic seasonal fruit jam.

Take a seat at the sweeping counter facing the genuine 1930s-era soda fountain, and watch their jerks work.

*815 Cole Street in Cole Valley*
*415-742-4932, theicecreambarsf.com*

**Tip:** *Be bold—ask for butterscotch ice cream in your root beer float!*

# TIP BACK A MARGARITA
## AT EL RIO

A remarkable mix of community space, all-inclusive watering hole, live music spot, and "jerk-free zone," El Rio's back patio is home to some of San Francisco's greatest afternoons that turned into evenings.

"Your mom would like us," El Rio says on their website, and it's true: everyone has a fantastic time at this bar, which attracts one of the most diverse crowds in the city.

Everyone is welcome at El Rio (even your dog!) as long as you're ready to have fun. There's a solid happy hour nearly every day, and live music almost every night. Outside food is welcome too, which might be necessary given the strength of their margaritas. So nothing's stopping you from grabbing a burrito at one of the many excellent area taquerias and then enjoying it at the bar, as you people-watch and make new friends.

You haven't been to San Francisco until you've been to El Rio.

*3158 Mission Street in the Mission*
*415-282-3325, elriosf.com*

# BRING A BIB
## FOR DUNGENESS SEASON

Dungeness crab season, which starts in mid-November, is practically an official four-month-long holiday in San Francisco, with lines of enthusiasts forming at numerous restaurants famous for making the most of the tasty crustaceans. Is this a juicy, messy meal? It is. Don't wear your favorite shirt and expect to stay spotless! Do expect savory goodness throughout the season, which ends in March.

**Here are some popular spots for Dungeness crab, with specialties noted.**

**Alioto's Restaurant** *(crab cioppino)*
*8 Fisherman's Wharf*
*415-673-0183, aliotos.com*

**Crustacean** *(drunken crab) and their sister spot*
**Thanh Long** *(roasted garlic crab)*
*1475 Polk Street in Nob Hill, 415-776-2722*
*or*
*4101 Judah Street in the Outer Sunset*
*415-665-1146, houseofan.com*

**PPQ Dungeness Island** *(roasted peppercorn crab)*
*2332 Clement Street*
*415-386-8266, ppqcrab.com*

**Swan Oyster Depot** *(half-cracked crab)*
*1517 Polk Street on Nob Hill*
*415-673-1101, sfswanoysterdepot.com*

# WAKE UP
## TO TARTINE'S MORNING BUN

See that early-morning line outside 600 Guerrero Street? Those are the pastry faithful, waiting for Tartine's buttery confection of croissant dough, sugar, cinnamon, and orange zest. Made from organic and local ingredients, all of Tartine Bakery and Café's offerings are addictively good (their bread is a hefty $9 a loaf and worth every penny), but the morning bun is the first thing people mention when you say "Tartine."

But if breakfast time has passed, Tartine is ready to blow you away with its peerless hot-pressed sandwiches. It's also a great dessert stop, as the tarts and cakes are the stuff of dreams. Grab a slice, or go for broke and order the full, nine-inch creation.

*600 Guerrero Street in the Mission*
*415-487-2600, tartinebakery.com*

**Tip:** *For the best selection of baked goods, check Tartine's website for opening times and get there early. When they run out of an item, that's often it for the day. You'll sleep when you're dead!*

# DO A DOSA OR TWO

San Francisco has two standout places to down dosai, the stuffed crepe of southern India typically filled with vegetables, sauces, meat, and more. Dosa, which has locations in both the Fillmore District and in the Mission, is an upscale introduction to the cuisine, suitable even for people who say that they "don't like Indian food." (Try the "prawn Frankie" dosa served at lunch). Udupi Palace, also located in the Mission, is a vegetarian fave and is known for its nuanced sauces and low price point.

**Dosa**
*995 Valencia Street in the Mission*
*415-642-3672*
*or*
*1700 Fillmore Street in the Fillmore District*
*415-441-3672, dosasf.com*

**Udupi Palace**
*1007 Valencia Street in the Mission*
*415-970-8000, udupipalacesanfrancisco.com*

# MUNCH ON
# A BEIGNET BRUNCH
## AT BRENDA'S FRENCH SOUL FOOD

Chef Brenda Buenviaje grew up in Louisiana, then came to San Francisco and took the food world by storm. The menu at her eponymous restaurant is an unusually comforting mix of her Sicilian, French, and Filipino roots.

Every meal at Brenda's is great, but her breakfast/brunch is a must, because that's when she serves her beignets, aka "New Orleans' favorite doughnut." You don't even have to choose between plain, chocolate, apple, or crawfish-stuffed, as Brenda offers a "flight" of all four.

Of course, you need to follow those beignets up with something! Try Brenda's Hangtown Fry (oysters, bacon, scallions, and eggs), her shrimp and cheddar grits (the tomato-bacon gravy is amazing), or her French toast with butter pecan sauce.

The best news is that she keeps on serving breakfast and brunch until 3 P.M., perfect for even the latest of risers.

*652 Polk Street in the Tenderloin*
*415-345-8100, frenchsoulfood.com*

**Tip:** *Brenda's doesn't take reservations, and waits at peak times can be long. Make an effort to go at off hours, and be patient. It's worth the wait.*

# FOLLOW YOUR NOSE
## TO THE BACON-WRAPPED HOT DOG CART

We're not kidding when we say "follow your nose," as this cart's wares perfume Mission Street between 16th and 24th Streets in the Mission District. Hop off BART at 16th Street, take a whiff of the air, and start walking.

Somewhere along the next eight blocks, it won't be long until you stumble upon a cart sizzling with one of the most decadent ways to blow your diet: the bacon-wrapped hot dog.

Order it naked or with jalapeños and other spicy fixin's. It's also a great way to soak up the booze/stave off a hangover if you've tied one too many on at one of the Mission's many great bars. See, it's practically health food when you think about it that way!

# DIP INTO
## A DESIGNER DONUT
## AT DYNAMO DONUT AND COFFEE

Your corner donut chain never thought of Dynamo's crazy flavor combinations, like Passion Fruit Milk Chocolate, Chocolate Rose, and Maple-Glazed Bacon Apple. But, somehow, they all work!

Check their website (dynamodonut.com) for the flavors of the day, and if you're in a rush you can even pre-order a day in advance, then pick up your choices the next day. But it's way more fun just to go with a couple of folks, take a seat in the charming back patio, order a bunch of the excellent coffee and donuts, and share so everyone can try all of Dynamo's remarkable offerings. No fighting!

*2760 24th Street in the Mission*
*415-920-1978, dynamodonut.com*

**Tip:** *Like many of San Francisco's restaurants, Dynamo is closed on Mondays.*

# MUSIC AND ENTERTAINMENT

# MAKE LIKE A CULTURE VULTURE
## AT THE OPERA, BALLET, OR SYMPHONY

A night at the opera, the ballet, or the symphony (under the direction of the estimable Michael Tilson Thomas) is always a treat, with expectations for excellence most often met. Order tickets in advance or show up at the last minute to see if any primo seats (or maybe a place to stand at the back) have been released.

**San Francisco Opera**
*301 Van Ness Avenue in the Civic Center*
*415-864-3330, sfopera.com*

**San Francisco Ballet**
*301 Van Ness Avenue in the Civic Center*
*415-861-5600, sfballet.org*

**San Francisco Symphony**
*201 Van Ness Avenue in the Civic Center*
*415-864-6000, sfsymphony.org*

**Tip:** *If cabaret is your thing, see who is on tap at Feinstein's at the Nikko, the 140-seat venue that draws many a top entertainer. See hotelnikkosf.com/feinsteins.*

# JOIN THE JAZZ AND BLUES CROWD
## AT THE SFJAZZ CENTER

In the 1940s and 1950s, San Francisco's Fillmore District was known as the "Harlem of the West," and Louis Armstrong, John Coltrane, Ella Fitzgerald, Billie Holiday, and Charlie Parker all played in the clubs lining Fillmore Street.

Today, many jazz and blues enthusiasts head to the gleaming new SFJAZZ Center in Hayes Valley, said to be the biggest jazz presenter on the West Coast and the first stand-alone structure in the country built specifically for jazz. Acoustics, sight lines, and just the right vibe all were considered when constructing the intimate concert hall that now welcomes the best of the best in jazz, Latin, and global music.

*JazzTimes* notes: "The building is breathtaking, a human-scale glass box that sweeps you in off the sidewalk. Jazz has an enviable new home in San Francisco."

The center also sponsors a twelve-day jazz festival in mid-June.

**SFJAZZ Center**
*201 Franklin Street in Hayes Valley*
*866-920-5299, sfjazz.org*

# FIND YOUR NEW FAVOITE BAND
## AT NOISEPOP

This indie music, arts, and film festival is over two decades strong, and in that time, fans have seen acts as varied as Yoko Ono, X, and Antony and the Johnsons. Offering old favorites as well as the most cutting-edge new artists, this fest has acts in all stages of the rock-and-roll life cycle, set in some of San Francisco's greatest and most historic venues.

But NoisePop is more than just music: during the festival, there's also a series of music-related films, multiple gallery shows of visual arts, and a number of happy hours for you and your NoisePop pals to mix and mingle. You're sure to come away from NoisePop a little bit deafer, but a lot more inspired.

Typically held the third week of February.

*noisepop.com*

# EXPAND YOUR CINEMATIC HORIZONS
## AT INDIEFEST

In an era where attendees at "independent" film festivals are plied with gift bags and sponsored sodas before a blockbuster-to-be unspools, SF IndieFest keeps things refreshingly rough and real.

Founded in 1998 by a guy and his credit cards, the more-than-a-week-long festival draws tens of thousands with raw, truly independent gems you will not see anywhere else on earth. Luminaries like Gregg Araki and Bruce Campbell rub shoulders with film fans at this down-to-earth showcase of alternative and subversive cinema.

IndieFest has been so successful that it's even spawned two spin-off fests, DocFest, an annual festival dedicated to documentary films, and Another Hole in the Head Genre Film Festival, a yearly celebration of horror, sci-fi, and fantasy cinema. No matter the fest, expect to see haunting works you won't find anywhere else.

**IndieFest:** *typically held the second week of February*
**DocFest:** *typically held the second week of June*
**Another Hole in the Head:** *typically held the first week of December*

*sfindie.com*

# INHABIT OTHER REALITIES
## AT *BEACH BLANKET BABYLON*

Over the past forty years, almost six million people have filed into Club Fugazi to see *Beach Blanket Babylon*—the city's own rowdy musical revue—and most of them have come out laughing! The show spoofs everyone who is somebody (or wants to be) and does it all with vastly talented voices, delightful costumes, and ginormous hats that must be seen to be believed. The script changes all the time, playing off pop culture and reacting to breaking news and new faux pas and foibles committed by the rich and famous on this continent and others.

Not bad for a show that originally opened for a six-week run and now is said to be the longest-running musical revue in theater history. And where did the cast celebrate the fortieth anniversary of the show? At city hall, surrounded by fans from all walks of life.

Just go—it's good, and good for a laugh!

### *Beach Blanket Babylon* at Club Fugazi
*678 Green Street in North Beach*
*415-421-4222, beachblanketbabylon.com*

**Tip:** *Other San Francisco theaters offer poignant dramas, powerful solo shows, and touring Broadway musicals. Half-price tickets for some shows can be found at TIX Bay Area at the west end of Union Square at 350 Powell Street. (tixbayarea.com)*

# TAKE IN A FLICK
## AT THE CASTRO THEATRE

Built in 1922, the Castro is one of the only movie palaces from the 1920s that is still in operation. Designed by noted architect Timothy L. Pflueger, the theater has since been updated with comfy contemporary seating, a cutting-edge sound system, and a new screen. But the venue's mighty Wurlitzer pipe organ remains and is played before every screening.

The Castro's programming is diverse. Each week its stage and screen is home to a mix of mainstream releases, art house classics, film fest picks, and other special events. Don't miss their sing-along events for films like *The Sound of Music*, *The Wizard of Oz*, and Disney classics, when everyone in the packed theater raises their voice in song. It's a religious experience.

*429 Castro Street in the Castro*
*415-621-6120, castrotheatre.com*

**Tip:** *The seats on the main floor are newer and comfier, but how often do you get to watch a movie from the balcony these days? Head up the stairs at the right or the left of the entrance to watch your movie in true style.*

# LET YOUR HAIR DOWN
## AT A GOLDEN GATE PARK MUSIC FESTIVAL

While Golden Gate Park is home to dozens of festivals and events every year, there are two must-see events that draw locals and visitors alike. Outside Lands and Hardly Strictly Bluegrass are both nationally renowned festivals that pack thousands into the park on their respective weekends.

Both fests are a lot more than music, as San Francisco's food scene comes out to serve the masses in deliciously inventive style. With diverse lineups and multiple stages, both festivals are a see-and-be-seen scene. (Say that three times fast!) One significant differentiator: while Outside Lands tickets (which can run you hundreds of dollars) typically sell out months in advance, Hardly Strictly Bluegrass is a free event, open to all.

### Outside Lands
*Typically the second weekend in August*
*sfoutsidelands.com*

### Hardly Strictly Bluegrass
*Typically the first weekend in October*
*hardlystrictlybluegrass.com*

**Tip:** *No matter how sunny it is in the morning, when the fog rolls in at night, Golden Gate Park gets really chilly. Toss a toasty sweater in your festival bag, and try hard not to look superior when you pass all the shivering folks in tank tops at the end of the night.*

# CRACK UP
## AT THE PUNCH LINE

For thirty-two years, the country's best comics have been killing at the Punch Line, San Francisco's only full-time live comedy venue. Stars like Robin Williams, Ellen DeGeneres, Rosie O'Donnell, Drew Carey, Chris Rock, and Dana Carvey got their start at the Punch Line, cementing the venue's reputation among comics as the place to go to hone your craft.

And even now, the Punch Line keeps going strong, featuring the best in national stand-up, acts on the brink of stardom, and showcases of early-stage talent. There's a full bar (with a two-drink minimum) and a kitchen rolling out foolproof bar food during every show.

*444 Battery Street in the Financial District*
*415-397-7573, punchlinecomedyclub.com*

# HEAR SOUND SCULPTED
## AT AUDIUM

Since the 1950s, composer Stan Schaff says he's been seeking to "explore the spatial musical dimension." This search reached its logical conclusion with Audium, a 169-speaker performance space "constructed specifically for sound movement, utilizing the entire environment as a compositional tool."

At 8:30 every Friday and Saturday night, audience members take their seats in concentric circles as a tape performer sends sounds rocketing through speakers in sloping walls, a floating floor, and a suspended ceiling.

As Schaff says, audience members will "see with their ears and feel with their bodies sounds as images, dreams, and memories." You have never heard anything like this.

*1616 Bush Street in Pacific Heights*
*415-771-1616, audium.org*

**Tip:** *Ticket sales at the door are cash only,*
*and no kids under twelve are allowed.*

# LIVE ROCK HISTORY
## AT THE FILLMORE

There are lots of great venues to hear live music in San Francisco! But the rich history at the Fillmore makes all others pale in comparison: it's truly one in a million. Built in 1912 as a dance hall, the venue was briefly a roller rink before 1952, when some of the biggest names in African American music started playing shows there. A bohemian hangout through the '50s, a hippie hotspot in the '60s—if you're anyone in music, you've played the Fillmore.

Proof of that assertion covers the Fillmore's walls, which are papered nearly floor to ceiling with iconic posters advertising the Fillmore dates for some of the biggest names in music. Head upstairs to their bar/restaurant and balcony for even more concert art, and eavesdrop as old-timers recount their experiences at those long-ago shows.

Check the online calendar to see who's playing or just buy tickets to whatever's next. Who knows, you might discover your new favorite band.

*1805 Geary Boulevard in the Fillmore District*
*415-346-3000, thefillmore.com*

# FIT IN A FREE SHOW
## AT AMOEBA MUSIC

There it sits at the western end of Haight Street, a converted bowling alley now filled with a massive selection of music, movies, and memorabilia. But while we urge you to shop to your heart's content, there's an even better deal: multiple times a week, you can see national acts performing on the in-store stage, at no charge whatsoever. Feel free to dance like no one's watching in the aisles; just be ready to scoot if you're blocking someone's CD shopping.

Not in the mood for a show? Then hit Amoeba's used section for some of the best deals you can imagine on music and movies. Before you say "who buys CDs and DVDs these days?" you should check out their selection: there's a lot of stuff in their bins that you can't find digitally. Worth a look!

*1855 Haight Street in the Upper Haight*
*415-831-1200, amoeba.com*

# RECREATION AND SPORT

# TAKE A CITY TOUR

Confused about what's where in this compact city full of enticing neighborhoods, places of natural beauty, and iconic attractions? Go on a city tour! Hop on a big open-top bus, squeeze into a tiny vehicle that seats just two, ride on a vintage fire truck, or take to the skies in a helicopter to help learn your way around.

For fares and departure points, check with the companies.

1. **San Francisco Sightseeing** (415-434-8687 or sanfranciscosightseeing.com), City Sightseeing (415-440-8687 or city-sightseeing.us), **Gray Line** (415-353-5310 or grayline.com/things-to-do/united-states/san-francisco), and **Tower Tours** (415-345-8687 or towertours.com) all offer 3½-hour bus tours.

2. **San Francisco Comprehensive Shuttle Tours** specializes in in-depth five- and nine-hour shuttle tours that include a ferry ride. (866-991-8687 or sanfranshuttletours.com)

3. Feeling adventurous? Rent a **GoCar**, a gas-powered, open-top mini-coupe with a loaded GPS. (800-914-6227 or gocartours.com/our-tour-cities/san-francisco)

4. Climb aboard a vintage fire truck for a ride from Fisherman's Wharf across the Golden Gate Bridge and back with **San Francisco Fire Engine Tours**. (415-333-7077 or fireenginetours.com)

5. **San Francisco Helicopters** offers flight tours of twenty minutes or longer. (800-400-2404 or sfhelicopters.com/vista)

> **Tip:** *Bring layers, because San Francisco is likely chillier than you imagined, especially in the summer.*
> *If you forget, shops are standing by to fill your fleece needs.*

# CROSS OVER THE
## GOLDEN GATE BRIDGE

Drive-by sightseeing is fine for some spots, but to really appreciate the Golden Gate Bridge and the adjacent scenic vistas, see it on foot. The 1.7-mile hike is an easy walk, and on a clear day, the experience will take your breath away. (On a cold, foggy day, about all you will see is your breath.)

Look east to Alcatraz Island and the city's skyline, look west to the Pacific Ocean, look down and you may catch a glimpse of harbor porpoises darting in the waves. At the center of the bridge, you are 220 feet above the waters of the famous Golden Gate, which is the name of the three-mile-long strait that flows into San Francisco Bay.

**Tip:** *Wondering where to park?*
*See goldengatebridge.org/visitors/directions.php.*

# LEAVE THE DRIVING
## TO MUNI

If you've got the time, we've got Muni. The impressive fleet of public transit vehicles includes buses, light rail, cable cars, and historic streetcars to take you wherever you want to go. Muni has stops and stations in every neighborhood, and some Muni stations also serve BART, aka the Bay Area Rapid Transit system.

Buy a Clipper Card (which allows you to add as much or as little transit money as you'd like and can also be used on BART and other Bay Area transit agencies) or bring cash—no change is given on Muni.

Cash fare for all buses, light rail, and historic streetcars is $2.25 for adults ($2 with a Clipper Card), 75 cents for seniors 65 and older and youths 5 to 17, and free for kids under 4. If paying in cash, make sure to get a transfer (it proves you paid) and ride again free within a ninety-minute period. Pick up a Street and Transit Map at locations all over town or download a mobile app for schedules.

*415-701-2311, sfmta.com*

> **Tip:** *San Francisco also has taxis and car services, including Uber, Lyft, and Sidecar.*

# FROLIC
## IN GOLDEN GATE PARK

There isn't enough to do in Golden Gate Park—there is too much! This 1,017-acre urban playground offers plenty of green space and outstanding special attractions. Stroll through the elegant Conservatory of Flowers, commune with a bison herd, relax with a beverage at the Japanese Tea House, paddle a boat on placid Stow Lake, or ride a carousel built in 1914.

You can also pay homage to William Shakespeare in a garden filled with plants mentioned in the Bard's works or visit a pair of Dutch-style windmills by the sea. When John F. Kennedy Drive is closed to traffic on Sundays, bike, skate, or just take a walk along the eastern half of the road, where chances are you'll find swing dancers at 8th Avenue near the museums and roller skating, funk/disco dancers at 6th Avenue.

Park boundaries are Fulton Street, Lincoln Way, the Great Highway along Ocean Beach, and Stanyan Street.

*415-831-2700, golden-gate-park.com*

**Tip:** *Wanna-be archers, listen up! Nine hay bales make up the city's only archery range, on Fulton Street between 45th and 46th Avenues in Golden Gate Park. (415-751-2776)*

# HOP ABOARD A BOAT
## IN SAN FRANCISCO BAY

Big boats, little boats, even amphibious boats are all waiting to take you out on San Francisco Bay, whether you've got just an hour to spend or you're up for a leisurely dinner cruise. Call for current rates and boarding times. Sailing tours and private yacht charters are also available.

1. The **Blue and Gold Fleet** and the **Red and White Fleet** both offer sixty- to ninety-minute cruises on large excursion boats with indoor and outdoor seating. Some trips go to Sausalito, Tiburon, and Angel Island.

**The Blue and Gold Fleet**
*Pier 41 at Fisherman's Wharf*
*415-773-1188, blueandgoldfleet.com*

**The Red and White Fleet**
*Pier 43 at Fisherman's Wharf*
*415-673-2900, redandwhite.com*

2. Zip around the bay on a thirty-minute **RocketBoat** cruise, offered from mid-May through the end of October, weather permitting. Children must be forty inches tall to ride. Folks in the front and middle seats are less likely to get wet.

*Pier 39 at Fisherman's Wharf*
*415-773-1188, blueandgoldfleet.com/rocketboat*

3. A four-course dinner, live entertainment, and dancing can make for a romantic evening on one of **Hornblower**'s dinner cruise yachts.

*San Francisco Pier 3*
*The Embarcadero at Washington Street*
*415-438-8300, hornblower.com/port/category/sf+diningcruises*

4. A raucous ninety-minute trip (You'll sing! You'll even quack!) with **Ride the Ducks** takes you through the streets of San Francisco and right into the water. These modern-day replicas of the World War II amphibious boats are certified by the Coast Guard.

*2766 Taylor Street at Fisherman's Wharf*
*877-887-8225, sanfrancisco.ridetheducks.com*

5. Fishing boats docked just west of Fisherman's Wharf in the afternoon offer quick trips to the **Golden Gate Bridge** and back at bargain prices. Bring a jacket—it's always colder on the water than on shore.

**Tip:** *Eager to see the bay from a kayak?*
*Call City Kayak at 415-294-1050 (citykayak.com) or San Francisco Kayak & Adventures at 415-787-2628 (sfkayak.com).*

# WHEEL YOUR WAY
## AROUND TOWN

See yourself zipping through San Francisco on a bike? Self-guided bike tours and guided rides are available from several companies. Types of bikes and tour rates vary, so check with each company.

### Bay City Bike Rentals and Tours
*1325 Columbus Avenue*
*415-346-2453, baycitybike.com*

### Bike and Roll
*899 Columbus Avenue*
*415-229-2000, bikeandroll.com/sanfrancisco*

### Blazing Saddles Bike Tours
*433 Mason Street*
*415-202-8888, blazingsaddles.com*

### Streets of San Francisco
*370 Linden Street*
*415-448-7673, sosfbiketours.com*

> **Tip:** *If you want to ride through San Francisco city parks, Parkwide is the official concessionaire, with five rental stands around town. (415-671-8989 or parkwide.com)*

# SPEED OFF
## ON A SEGWAY

If you're a stand-up guy or gal, book a Segway tour. The Electric Tour Company and City Segway Tours both offer several guided Segway tours, including outings that spend time on Alcatraz Island. Segway SF Bay provides a map so you may explore on your own.

All three companies provide orientation classes before you set off. At Segway SF Bay, the lesson is free and if you don't like the Segway after all, you can go find a bus tour, with no obligation.

You must be twelve or older and weigh at least one hundred pounds to ride. Also, Segway tours are not recommended for pregnant women, some guests seventy and older, or people with some mobility issues.

**The Electric Tour Company**
*757 Beach Street near Fisherman's Wharf*
*or*
*82 Hagiwara Tea Garden Drive in Golden Gate Park*
*(look for the tent)*
*415-474-3130, electrictourcompany.com*

**City Segway Tours**
*333 Jefferson St.*
*Suite 123, sanfrancisco.citysegwaytours.com*

**Segway SF Bay**
*1263 20th Avenue*
*415-716-9910, segwaysfbay.com*

# TALK TO THE TREES
## IN THE BOTANICAL GARDEN

You can sit in a peaceful redwood grove, watching the play of light on the soft forest floor and listening to the trickling of water in a nearby creek—without ever leaving the city!

Where is that possible in this bustling metropolis? The San Francisco Botanical Garden boasts a towering stand of hundred-year-old redwoods surrounded by plants typically found in the larger forests farther north on the coast. This relaxing, sun-dappled spot provides plenty of benches where you may sit and just be with the trees. The scent is positively intoxicating, and even the sounds of city traffic are hushed here.

Refreshed by the quietude in the grove, take time to explore the rest of the fifty-five-acre garden, which is home to more than eight thousand different plants from around the world. Maps are available at the entrance.

*1199 9th Avenue in Golden Gate Park*
*415-661-1316, sfbotanicalgarden.org*

# EXPERIENCE BASEBALL
## SAN FRANCISCO STYLE

If you plan to catch a Giants game at beautiful AT&T Park, know that some (rare) days it's sunny and hot like in other baseball towns, but many days and most nights, a few hours spent with our 2010 and 2012 World Series champions includes brisk winds, wispy fog, and circling seagulls. Bring layers, and maybe warm gloves. Really.

Before the first pitch, at the seventh-inning stretch, or whenever the mood strikes, stroll around the waterfront promenade for breathtaking views of the ferries and container ships in the bay and the kayaks in McCovey Cove. (Look for the tiny pirate ship!) The kids can go down the slide inside the giant Coke bottle. The whole family can share an order of our famous garlic fries. Then buy a Ghirardelli hot fudge sundae and eat it in the retired cable car above right-center field.

**AT&T Park**
*24 Willie Mays Plaza in SoMa (South of Market)*
*415-972-1800, sfgiants.com*

# CATCH A FLY-BY
## OF WILD PARROTS

Before you see them, you'll hear them—our squawking and screeching parrots, flying first this way and then that, wheeling high above the buildings near Telegraph Hill, in Cole Valley, around the Embarcadero, over Laurel Village, and in the Presidio—and anywhere else they choose to fly.

These wild parrots are smaller than the seagulls, ravens, and raptors soaring above you, and besides, they're bright green. We've seen as few as six flying together and as many as twenty or more. Talk about a satisfying celebrity sighting!

The birds are descendants of the red-headed conures featured in *The Wild Parrots of Telegraph Hill*, the moving documentary about an unemployed musician and his relationship with the wild parrots in the city. If you miss this exhilarating display of color and sound in real time, get the movie, which was released in 2003.

# WIND YOUR WAY
## ALONG AN URBAN TRAIL

Walk, walk, walk! We all do a lot of it in San Francisco, and not every hike requires climbing our steep hills—but those challenges are available here as well as easy flat paths. You decide.

1. The four-mile Coastal Trail along Ocean Beach is for those who crave the sights and sounds of the sea. Start at the Cliff House Restaurant on the Great Highway and head south to Fort Funston.

2. Glen Canyon Park, a microcosm of wilderness, covers about seventy acres and stretches through three residential neighborhoods, so carve out whatever sort of walk you want. The steepest rise is 250 feet.

3. The Golden Gate Promenade, a stretch of just over four miles, follows the shoreline from the Marina to Fort Point, which provides an amazing view of the south tower of the Golden Gate Bridge.

4. Up for an extended stroll in an urban setting? Start where Market Street begins in the Castro and follow this "Path of Gold" for about three miles to the famous Ferry Building.

5. Walking trails abound in the Presidio, with hikes from under one mile to more than four, ranging from easy to moderate. Watch for Andy Goldsworthy's organic art and many a scenic vista along the way.

6. Eager to climb higher? Walk to the top of Twin Peaks, two 922-foot-tall hills smack in the center of San Francisco. The view of the city is spectacular! For hikes in more natural environments, scale wooded Mount Sutro or Mount Davidson, both nearby.

# WATCH THE WAVES
## ON THE PACIFIC OCEAN

When sightseeing takes its toll, the perfect antidote is simply to sit and stare at the water. Here are primo spots for doing just that:

**Crissy Field:** After you stroll on the beach or along the path, after you check out the shorebirds in the marsh, after you grab coffee or tea at the Warming Hut, go sit on the low wall and keep track of the water flowing in and out of the Golden Gate. (parksconservancy.org/visit/park-sites/crissy-field.html)

**Fort Funston:** You can hang glide, you can hike, and you can go horseback riding here—or you can walk a few steps from the parking lot and relax on the wooden deck perched on a bluff two hundred feet above the beach. (parksconservancy.org/visit/park-sites/fort-funston.html)

**Lands End:** Hang out high above where the Pacific Ocean meets the strait known as the Golden Gate. The water is at least three different colors here on the city's rocky northwestern corner, and you can watch the play of light on the waves. (parksconservancy.org/visit/park-sites/lands-end.html)

# GO GAGA
## FOR YERBA BUENA GARDENS

The Yerba Buena Gardens is the yin to this city's pulsating yang. Surrounded by museums, an urban movie theater, and a busy convention center, this lovely two-square-block public park is a great place to relax on a bench next to a butterfly garden, ice skate (indoors), ride a historic carousel, attend a lecture, or enjoy a calming cup of tea.

Stop to reflect by the rushing waters of the Martin Luther King Jr. Memorial, spend time with the kids at the Children's Garden, and explore the other gardens, including the Oche Wat Te Ou, a tribute to the native Ohlone Indians.

Before you leave the gardens, check the events schedule at the Yerba Buena Center for the Arts, which offers cutting-edge visual arts displays, performances, and films, all presented from diverse cultural and artistic perspectives. (See ybca.org.)

*750 Howard Street in SoMa (South of Market)*
*415-820-3550, yerbabuenagardens.com*

# PEER OFF
## THE END OF PIER 7

For a different view of San Francisco, take a short walk on this 840-foot pier located between Broadway and Pacific Streets on the Embarcadero—one of the few public-access piers in the city. Look back at the buildings that make up the city's famous skyline, including the Ferry Building, the Transamerica Pyramid, and Coit Tower. Look out at the water and enjoy the view of the Bay Bridge. From dusk until dawn, that bridge showcases "Bay Lights," a dramatic light sculpture designed by world-renowned artist Leo Villareal.

The wooden deck, ornamental iron rails, and comfortable benches make the pier a welcoming place, so you won't be alone. Pier 7 draws office workers enjoying a break, tourists, couples in love, joggers, and people who come to fish. The haul may include crab, bat rays, flounder, sole, or halibut. The bycatch is always a few moments of peace.

# MEET THE STATE MAMMAL
## AT THE ZOO

Kachina and Kiona, orphaned sisters originally from Montana, live in Grizzly Gulch at the San Francisco Zoo, the oldest and largest zoo in northern California. Our grizzlies wrestle and play in their very own meadow, and you can watch them chow down at 11:30 A.M. every day. Before you move on to the next exhibit, read about the late Monarch, the grizzly whose image appears on the California state flag.

The Lemur Forest is another highlight at the hundred-acre zoo, where four species of these lively primates live among the trees. Koalas also live at our zoo, and sometimes they even wake up and blink at visitors. The Magellanic penguins never fail to amuse. Stop by Penguin Island at 10:30 A.M. or 3:30 P.M. to enjoy the birds' antics at feeding time. (The seagulls always do!)

Also, the historic carousel and a spacious playground modeled after three habitats are magnets for kids.

*1 Zoo Road in the Outer Sunset*
*415-753-7080, sfzoo.org*

**Tip:** *To you, that fiberglass sign on a median outside the zoo may just look like a seven-foot-high dog's head topped with a chef's hat, but that's San Francisco Landmark No. 254. All hail the much-loved, now defunct Doggie Diner!*

# MINGLE WITH LOCALS
## AT FESTIVALS AND FAIRS

Want to get to know those of us who live here? You'll find a lot of us in all our diverse glory at the many street fairs, parades, and festivals. At most events, expect food, music, and plenty of arts and crafts booths selling handmade items. Most street fairs are free, though some accept donations. Here are just a few of our bigger festivals and fairs:

1. **Lunar New Year Parade:** February in Chinatown
2. **St. Patrick's Day Parade:** The Saturday nearest to March 17 on Market Street
3. **Cherry Blossom Festival:** Mid-April in Japantown's Peace Plaza
4. **Asian Heritage Street Celebration:** Mid-May in the Little Saigon neighborhood
5. **San Francisco Carnaval:** Last weekend in May in the Mission
6. **San Francisco Ethnic Dance Festival:** Four weekends in June at the Yerba Buena Center for the Arts
7. **Union Street Eco-Urban Festival:** First weekend in June in Cow Hollow
8. **Haight-Ashbury Street Fair:** First Sunday in June in Haight-Ashbury
9. **North Beach Festival:** Second weekend in June in North Beach
10. **San Francisco LGBT Pride Celebration:** Last weekend in June, all over San Francisco
11. **AIDS Walk:** Mid-July, across San Francisco
12. **Cole Valley Fair:** Last Sunday in September in Cole Valley
13. **Castro Street Fair:** First Sunday in October in the Castro
14. **Day of the Dead:** November 2 in the Mission

# GO WHALE WATCHING

Mighty blue whales, the biggest creatures ever to live on the planet, often stop for lunch off the continental shelf near the Farallon Islands, just twenty-seven miles from the city. Just how big are blue whales? Real big: they can measure from ninety to one hundred feet long and weigh up to two hundred tons.

You can go see these giants, along with their friends the humpbacks and the grays, on a whale watch that departs from San Francisco. Weather permitting, full-day trips take place on most Saturdays and Sundays for much of the year. You may spot up to twenty different species of marine mammals on your trip—but because this is nature and not Disneyland, you may hit a day when there is a dearth of marine life.

That said, a day on a boat is always a good day!

### Oceanic Society
*415-256-9604 or 800-326-7491, oceanicsociety.org*

*Boat departs at 8 A.M. from San Francisco Marina Yacht Harbor at 3950 Scott Street and returns at 4 P.M. Free parking. Age minimum is ten and an adult must accompany youths under fifteen. Advance reservations required.*

### SF Bay Whale Watching
*415-331-6267, sfbaywhalewatching.com*

*Boat departs at 8 A.M. from Pier 39 at Fisherman's Wharf and returns between 2 and 3 P.M. No children under three allowed on the boat. Advance reservations required.*

> **Tip:** *Birdwatchers will want to make the trip in May, June, or early July, when hundreds of thousands of seabirds, including tufted puffins, nest on the Farallon Islands.*

# SMILE
## FOR THE CAMERA OBSCURA

Don't ask us to explain the concept behind the giant camera obscura just above Ocean Beach (it's all about light waves and pinholes and maybe a mirror), but do go see this rare optical device's live panoramic images of nearby Seal Rock, magnified seven times.

Leonardo da Vinci designed the first camera obscura (not to be confused with the Scottish indie pop band of the same name), and the one here today (the third, history tells us) was built in 1946, part of the Playland at the Beach amusement park. Today it is a national landmark and on the National Register of Historic Places.

Anyway, you can't miss the current camera obscura, just a few steps below Cliff House—it's shaped like a giant camera. Whether or not you grasp the concept, you'll enjoy the experience!

*1096 Point Lobos in the Outer Richmond*
*415-750-0415, giantcamera.com*

**Tip:** *Afterward, walk back up to the historic Cliff House*
*for a meal or a smooth-as-silk pear martini*
*as you enjoy the spectacular ocean view.*

# RUN FOR YOUR LIFE

With our steep hills, multiple microclimates, and stunning views, San Francisco is a uniquely rewarding and challenging city to run in. Populated by health and fitness enthusiasts, this town offers a road race almost any weekend (check runningintheusa.com).

These four are on every San Franciscan's bucket list—why not add them to yours?

1. **Bay to Breakers** is the oldest consecutively run annual foot race in the world, dating from May 1912. Around seventy thousand people—some serious runners, some in costume and ready to party, some wearing nothing at all—cover the 7.46 miles from the Embarcadero to Ocean Beach. Third Saturday in May, baytobreakers.com

2. The **San Francisco Marathon** might be the toughest marathon you ever run, with hills that will break your heart, but there are also two half marathons and a 5K for the more leisurely among us. Then again, in the double marathon, runners tackle the entire course in reverse starting at midnight and then begin again at the starting line at 5:30 A.M. Last weekend in July, thesfmarathon.com

3. In **Bridge to Bridge**, runners cover a 5K or 12K course along our gorgeous waterfront, running from the beautiful Bay Bridge to the iconic Golden Gate Bridge. First Sunday in October, rhodyco.com/event-schedule

4. The **Escape from Alcatraz Triathlon** begins with a 1.5-mile swim from Alcatraz Island in the icy waters of San Francisco Bay. Next you hop on a bike for an eighteen-mile ride through Golden Gate Park, and then you run eight miles to the Marina Green. This is a serious race for serious athletes, but completing it successfully gives you bragging rights for life. First weekend in June, escapefromalcatraztriathlon.com

# STRETCH OUT
## ON A WORLD-FAMOUS LABYRINTH

One of San Francisco's most remarkable collective experiences is Yoga on the Labyrinth. Hundreds of people from all over the world come to Grace Cathedral's lovely and iconic indoor labyrinth every Tuesday night for a gentle hatha yoga class accompanied by a rotating list of guest musicians.

Expect a diverse group of practitioners, young and old, experienced and first-timers, and people of all religions and races. This is not your typical yoga night at the YMCA!

Class starts at 6:15 P.M., but it's suggested you arrive early to beat the crowd. Bring your own mat and props, and dress warm, as even on pleasant nights, the cathedral can get cold. There's a suggested donation of $10–$20, but no one is turned away for lack of funds.

*1100 California Street on Nob Hill*
*415-857-4913, labyrinthyoga.com*

# CULTURE
# AND HISTORY

# WALK THIS WAY
## ON A NEIGHBORHOOD TOUR

You'll see them on the city streets, small groups of people staring intently at houses, statues, storefronts, or historic plaques. What are they doing? They're on one of the many walking tours offered here.

All ninety of the City Guides Tours are free, though donations are welcome. Choose from such destinations as Chinatown, the Fillmore Jazz Preservation District, Golden Gate Park, the Castro, the Financial District, and North Beach by night.

### City Guides Tours
*415-557-4266, sfcityguides.org*

## These companies offer fee-based tours:

### Barbary Coast Trail
*415-454-2355, barbarycoasttrail.org*

### Crooks Tour of San Francisco
*415-713-3077, crookstour.com*

### Cruisin' the Castro Walking Tours
*415-255-1821, cruisinthecastro.com*

### Local Tastes of the City Tours
*415-665-0480, sffoodtour.com*

### Walk SF Tours
*415-779-5879, walksftours.com*

# BE DAZZLED
## BY CITY HALL'S DOME

You can't beat city hall—for excitement!

Marilyn Monroe and Joe DiMaggio were married here in 1954. Mayor George Moscone and Supervisor Harvey Milk were assassinated inside in 1978. The first same-sex weddings took place in 2004. And on any given day you may see naked people out front, protesting the recent ban on public nudity.

The five-story Beaux-Arts building spans two city blocks and boasts more than five hundred thousand square feet of open space. The glittering dome (gold leaf on special paint) is the fifth largest in the world, bigger even than the dome at the U.S. Capitol. Think about this: the Loma Prieta earthquake in 1989 twisted that dome four inches on its base!

Want to know more? Sign up in the lobby for a free tour at 10 A.M., noon, or 2 P.M., Monday through Friday, whenever city hall is open.

*1 Dr. Carlton B. Goodlett Place in the Civic Center*
*415-701-2311*

**TIP:** *Inside city hall, look for the bust of Harvey Milk that commemorates his service to San Francisco. Milk was the first openly gay man to be elected to public office in a major U.S. city.*

# CATCH A CABLE CAR

Our famous cable cars are part of the public transit system, but it's not so much getting from Point A to Point B as it is the romance (cue Tony Bennett) that lures most visitors. Three of the original cable car routes are in operation: the Powell-Hyde line, the Powell-Mason line, and the California line.

Cable car stops are posted along the routes, or you can hop aboard at the turn-arounds or the terminals (see sfcablecar.com/routes.html). A ride costs $6.

True cable car aficionados head for the Cable Car Museum, where you'll see the engines and winding wheels that pull the cables, assorted mechanical devices, historic photos, and three antique cars. Admission is free, and you can buy your own cable car bell at the museum shop.

*1201 Mason Street in Nob Hill*
*415-474-1887, cablecarmuseum.org*

# CHAT UP
## SOME PAINTED LADIES

If the Painted Ladies at 710–720 Steiner Street in Alamo Square could talk, would they complain about the traffic jams they cause? No—the residents along the square already do that, although big tour buses have been outlawed on the narrow street.

This famous row of colorful Victorian houses, built between 1892 and 1896, more likely would primp and pose and brag about being in the opening credits of *Full House*. Then they would convince you what a stunning picture they present against the skyline. And they are correct!

More lovingly restored Victorian row houses and Edwardian-era homes can be found in Haight-Ashbury, the Lower Haight, Pacific Heights, and other neighborhoods. And don't miss the beauties on the southwest corner of Waller Street at Masonic, just south of Haight-Ashbury.

**TIP:** *When you climb up the hill in Alamo Square Park to photograph the houses, watch where you step! Alamo Square Park is a popular pooping spot for pooches.*

# ROCK OUT ON ALCATRAZ

For maximum thrills at the famous former maximum-security prison, book the 2.5-hour Alcatraz Night Tour, which includes a narrated boat tour around the island, guided tours from the dock to the main prison building, and the riveting cell house audio tour. Plus, you get to watch the sunset from the island!

No matter what time you go, you need to know that Alcatraz Island is a national park with only one concessionaire permitted to dock there. Tickets routinely sell out weeks in advance, so book online in advance.

The boat leaves from Pier 33 on the Embarcadero. Wear comfortable walking shoes so you are prepared for the steep trail up to the cell house. Also, bring a snack and some water, because no food is sold on the boat or on the island.

*55 Francisco Street on the Embarcadero*
*415-981-7625, alcatrazcruises.com*

**Tip:** *We promised you thrills, and chills are also guaranteed on the night tour. After sundown, it's cold and windy on Alcatraz, so bundle up.*

# RAISE A GLASS
## AT THE CALIFORNIA ACADEMY OF SCIENCES

Want to get your science geek on without having to compete with kids to get close to Claude the albino alligator, the perky penguins, or the many other compelling exhibits at the California Academy of Sciences?

Every Thursday from 6 to 10 P.M., the academy holds NightLife, a cocktail party for adult visitors who want to roam through this amazing place, which houses the Steinhart Aquarium, the Morrison Planetarium, the Kimball Natural History Museum, and a four-story rainforest complete with live butterflies.

The weekly themed parties feature live music, visual art installations, food, and adult beverages. The biggest advantage? Admission is just $12, a considerable savings over the $29.95 fee for adults who visit during the day. You must be twenty-one or older, and ID is required.

*55 Music Concourse Drive in Golden Gate Park*
*415-379-8000, www.calacademy.org*

---

**Tip:** *For the full museum experience, go back during the day and bring the kids. Don't miss the giant Pacific octopus or the fifteen-foot-long yellow python and go up to the 2.5-acre Living Roof, where native California plants thrive.*

# A JEDI MASTER MEET
## IN THE PRESIDIO

"Do. Or do not. There is no try."

So says Yoda in *The Empire Strikes Back*, and that sums it up perfectly. Either you will go see a Yoda-sized bronze statue of the 26-inch-tall Jedi master himself or you will spend your time driving down what actually is only the third-crookedest street in San Francisco.

The statue of Yoda sits perched atop a fountain in front of Building B at Lucasfilm's headquarters at the Letterman Digital Arts Center at Chestnut and Lyon Streets in the Presidio.

If you visit—and if the Force is with you—you may get to pop into the lobby and see a life-size statue of Darth Vader and other artifacts from the *Star Wars* movies as well.

# SING A SEA CHANTEY
## AT HYDE STREET PIER

Liberate your inner old man (or woman) of the sea!

Join a free sea chantey sing-along at the San Francisco Maritime National Historical Park. The fun starts at 8 P.M. on the first Saturday of every month, and the singing goes on until midnight aboard the *C. A. Thayer* and the *Balclutha*, historic ships docked at the Hyde Street Pier. (Reservations are required. Call 415-561-7171.)

If you aren't the sort who sings and you choose to visit during the day, start at the Park Service Visitor Center at Jefferson and Hyde Streets. Next, check out the exhibits in the Maritime Museum at 900 Beach Street. Then head for the Hyde Street Pier, where you can explore several "floating museums," including a cargo ship, a steam ferry, and a paddlewheel tug.

**Park Service Visitor Center**
*499 Jefferson Street on Fisherman's Wharf*
*415-447-5000, nps.gov/safr/index.htm*

**TIP:** *After the sing-along, forego the pirates' traditional rum for an Irish coffee at the famous Buena Vista Café, just south of Hyde Street Pier.*

# STAND WHERE
# IT ALL BEGAN
## AT PORTSMOUTH SQUARE

You would never guess from the laid-back nature of the neighborhood now that Portsmouth Square was the city's first public square, established in the early nineteenth century as part of a small Mexican community called Yerba Buena. During the Mexican-American War, the U.S. seized the settlement in July 1846, and in 1847 the name was changed to San Francisco.

This square-block park at 733 Kearny Street in Chinatown now is home to three markers registered as California Historical Landmarks: one commemorating the first raising of the American flag on the square in 1846, one noting the eastern terminus of the Clay Street Hill Railroad Company, and one honoring the opening of the first public school in California in 1848.

Don't let the card games, busy children's playground, or the ugly parking garage here dissuade you. History was made on this very spot.

# MEANDER
## THROUGH OUR AMAZING MUSEUMS

Museums, large and small, feed the intellect and stimulate the senses at the same time—plus, you'll likely exit through a nifty gift shop.

1. Greet Ganesha at the top of the escalators, don't miss the teahouse, and stop in the meditation alcove at the **Asian Art Museum**, where all things Asian are on display.

200 Larkin Street in the Civic Center
415-581-3500, asianart.org

2. No joke—the **Cartoon Art Museum** houses six thousand pieces of original cartoon and animation art, including comic books, graphic novels, anime, and the funnies.

655 Mission Street in SoMa (South of Market)
415-227-8666, cartoonart.org

3. Pop in at the beautiful Yud Gallery at the **Contemporary Jewish Museum** and then stroll through the museum, which presents rotating exhibitions.

736 Mission Street in SoMa (South of Market)
415-655-7800, thecjm.org

4. The **de Young Museum** boasts a permanent collection of more than twenty-seven thousand works, including painting, sculpture, and decorative arts from the Americas, Africa, and Oceania.

50 Hagiwara Tea Garden Drive in Golden Gate Park
415-750-3600, deyoung.famsf.org

5. A cast of Rodin's *The Thinker* greets you at the stately entrance to the **Legion of Honor**, which is filled with European paintings, ancient art, and sculpture.

100 34th Avenue in the Outer Richmond
415-750-3600, legionofhonor.famsf.org

6. The distinctive voice of the late Maya Angelou introduces the stories in the slave narratives at the **Museum of the African Diaspora**, where art and technology are perfectly blended.

685 Mission Street in SoMa (South of Market)
415-358-7200, moadsf.org

7. The **Precita Eyes Muralists Association and Visitor Center** offers walking tours for visitors interested in the Mission neighborhood's colorful murals.

2981 24th Street at Harrison in the Mission
415-285-2287, precitaeyes.org/tours.html

8. The **Walt Disney Family Museum** appeals primarily to visitors interested in Walt Disney's life and in the art of animation. A theater shows classic Disney movies.

104 Montgomery Street in the Presidio
415-345-6800, waltdisney.org

**Authors' Note:** *The San Francisco Museum of Modern Art is closed for renovations through early 2016. See sfmoma.org to see where part of the collection is on display.*

**Tip:** *Find the elevator in the east end of the de Young Museum and ride up, up, up to the Hamon Tower Observation Floor for breathtaking panoramic views of Golden Gate Park, the Golden Gate Bridge, and many a San Francisco neighborhood.*

# HANG WITH THE BEATS
## AT THEIR MUSEUM

Are you Beat at heart? Are you of the opinion that the single most interesting thing that happened in 1955 was when Allen Ginsberg read his brilliant poem "Howl" on October 7 at the (now defunct) Six Gallery in San Francisco?

If so, the small but mighty Beat Museum awaits your visit. Original manuscripts, first editions, letters, and a handful of personal artifacts from Ginsberg, Jack Kerouac, Neil Cassady, Lawrence Ferlinghetti, and other gifted writers and artists from the Beat Generation are on display in this funky, one-of-a-kind repository.

Books, clothing, posters, and collectibles are available in the museum shop, but visitors are particularly encouraged to take away what founder and owner Jerry Cimino calls the spirit of the Beat Generation: "Tolerance, compassion and having the courage to live your individual truth."

*540 Broadway Street in North Beach*
*415-399-9626, www.kerouac.com*

**Tip:** *Literary aficionados who want to time travel even deeper will walk two blocks north to Caffe Trieste, the coffee shop at 601 Vallejo Street where members of the Beat Generation used to gather.*

# GET ALL HANDS-ON
## AT THE EXPLORATORIUM

The Exploratorium personifies "interactive," with some six hundred exhibits that encourage visitors of all ages to touch, to tinker, and to figure out how the world works, all while having fun.

With so much going on in one place, the Exploratorium can be overwhelming at first. The six galleries are Light and Sound, Human Behavior, Living Systems, Tinkering, the Outdoor Gallery, and the Bay Observatory Gallery. Just cruise through, and stop to play at any exhibit that grabs your attention.

A physicist and teacher founded this 330,000-square-foot museum, which the *New York Times* hailed as "the most important science museum to have opened since the mid-20th century." Don't miss the Exhibit Workshop, where creative types research, develop, and construct what's next for the museum. And check out the fog bridge installation outside.

Pier 15 on the Embarcadero at Green Street
415-528-4360, exploratorium.edu

**TIP:** *Tree people and other fans of the life sciences will want to head for the East Gallery, where parts of a fallen 250-foot-tall coastal Douglas fir illustrate what trees are all about.*

# SHOW THE KIDS A BARN OWL
## AT THE RANDALL MUSEUM

Peer at a barn owl, look at a lizard, or talk to a tortoise at the Randall Museum, a free, low-key attraction operated by the San Francisco Recreation and Parks Department. This little gem of a museum features live animals, a Tree House Room for toddlers, a full-size replica of an earthquake refugee shack, and a scale model of a red caboose for kids to climb on.

That reminds us—parents with kids obsessed by trains, take note: on Saturdays from 10 A.M. to 4 P.M., on the lower level of the museum, young visitors may guide model trains on the Golden Gate Model Railroad Club's train layout, one of the largest in the Bay Area.

No matter what day you visit, when you leave, don't miss the amazing view of the city from the grassy area at the back of the museum.

199 Museum Way in Corona Heights
415-554-9600, randallmuseum.org

# CONTEMPLATE THE WAY WE WERE
## AS SEEN IN WPA MURALS

Beautiful frescos and tile murals—all commissioned and paid for by the government as part of the Works Progress Administration's Federal Art Project—are on display here, all tenderly restored.

Alluring scenes of sea life (check out that sexy merman!) adorn the walls at the Aquatic Park Bathhouse near Fisherman's Wharf. Portraits of locals at work and play are at the Beach Chalet Restaurant, a pre-Depression-era structure across from Ocean Beach. Murals at Coit Tower in North Beach (you were going there anyway, right?) depict views of San Francisco Bay juxtaposed with scenes of political activism. Historical figures from the 1790s are shown in the murals at the Presidio Chapel. And twenty-nine panels in the atrium at Rincon Center in the Financial District show key moments in the history of California. Don't miss the mural titled *Finding Gold at Sutter's Mill*, a moment that changed California forever.

# MULL THE IMPERMANENCE OF MAN'S CREATIONS
## AT THE SUTRO BATHS

At the northernmost end of San Francisco's Ocean Beach, you'll see all that remains of the once-vast Sutro Baths, a massive, privately owned swimming pool complex that was the place to be in the late 1800s. It closed in the 1960s, and fell into ruin shortly thereafter when a mysterious fire destroyed what remained. Now, all that's left is a slight bit of the foundation of the once-majestic baths, which were constructed from 100,000 square feet of glass, 600 tons of iron, 3,500,000 board feet of lumber, and 10,000 cubic yards of concrete.

This haunting place by the sea really makes you think about what ruins your grandkids might be splashing around in one day.

**Point Lobos Avenue and Merrie Way in the Outer Richmond**
*(part of the Golden Gate National Recreation Area)*
*nps.gov/goga/historyculture/sutro-baths.htm*

**TIP:** *Keep your eye out for sea otters and seals,
as sometimes they swim in for a rest.*

# HAIL
## A HISTORIC STREETCAR

Not to be confused with the cable cars, the F Line's historic streetcars run from Market and Castro all the way up Market to Fisherman's Wharf. Less fraught and packed than the cable cars, these truly vintage vehicles from around the world are also a comparable bargain, as riders pay the standard Muni fare. You can learn more about these "museums in motion" at streetcar. org, and you can catch one at multiple stops along Market and up the Embarcadero.

# PAUSE
## AT A PLACE OF WORSHIP

Of course a city named after a saint would have somewhere for nearly every spiritual stripe to pause in reflection. Here are some notable places of worship.

Founded in June 1776, **Misión San Francisco de Asís**, also known as **Mission Dolores**, is said to be the oldest surviving structure in San Francisco. Stop by for Mass or just to soak up the history.

*3321 16th Street in the Castro*
*415-621-8203*

A service at **GLIDE Memorial United Methodist Church** is a life-changing experience, as Reverend Cecil Williams preaches his church's message of radical inclusion, justice, and love to a congregation made up of people of all beliefs and walks of life.

*330 Ellis Street in the Tenderloin*
*415-674-6000, glide.org*

The **San Francisco Zen Center**, one of the largest Buddhist sanghas outside Asia, welcomes students, visitors, lay people, priests, and monks, all shoulder to shoulder at daily meditation, regular monastic retreats, classes, and workshops. Newcomers are welcome at afternoon meditation.

*300 Page Street in Hayes Valley*
*415-863-3136, sfzc.org*

Officially established in 1850, **Congregation Emanu-El** is the largest Reform synagogue in northern California and the oldest congregation west of the Mississippi. Guests are welcome at Friday and Saturday Shabbat services, and the building is open for ten-minute drop-in tours.

*2 Lake Street in the Richmond*
*415-751-2535, www.emanuelsf.org*


**Saint Ignatius Church** is on the campus of the University of San Francisco, but its parishioners are a mix of families, singles, professionals, the blue-collared, and folks who look like they've never had to work a day in their lives. Mass is held every day of the week.

*650 Parker Avenue at the University of San Francisco*
*415-422-2188, stignatiussf.org*


**Grace Cathedral** is known for labyrinths, the columbarium, and its reputation for innovation and open-minded conversation. Visitors from around the globe come every day for multiple services and events.

*1100 California Street on Nob Hill*
*415-749-6300, gracecathedral.org*


Behind its plain storefront, **Saint John Coltrane African Orthodox Church** embraces a tight-knit community of worshippers who find religion through music, specifically, Coltrane's "A Love Supreme." All are welcome at Sunday services and the only requirement is that you get ready to sing, dance, and clap in praise.

*1286 Fillmore Street in the Western Addition*
*415-673-7144, coltranechurch.org*

# DANCE WITH A STAR
## ON TREASURE ISLAND

*Bliss Dance*—a 45-foot-tall, 7,000-pound steel and mesh statue—was originally built by Marco Cochrane for the 2010 Burning Man, but now she rocks out on the Great Lawn, near 9th Street and Avenue of the Palms, on Treasure Island, a former naval base that is considered part of the city though it's situated in San Francisco Bay.

Some say *Bliss Dance* is the largest female nude sculpture in the country. Who knows? But we promise that this graceful statue, portrayed in motion, is awesome in every sense of the word. Go see *Bliss Dance* during the day and you can also revel in the view of San Francisco across the water. Go at night, and the statue is lit from within with a thousand LEDs.

We dare you not to dance—even though *Bliss Dance* will be watching.

**Tip:** Burning Man began at Baker Beach in San Francisco in 1986.

# MAKE LIKE
## STEVE MCQUEEN IN *BULLITT*

If you haven't seen Steve McQueen's 1968 classic action thriller *Bullitt,* put this book down and go watch it now.

OK, now that you're back, it's time to relive his iconic car chase across the city. While it's impossible to retrace the exact route of the chase, as far-flung streets were cobbled together for cinematic reasons, visit the map at goo.gl/E1pAMr to see all the locations McQueen tore through.

Then hop in your car (bonus points if it's a Mustang) and—safely—follow in his footsteps.

And *Bullitt* isn't the only movie set in San Francisco that's worth tracking: if you're a Dirty Harry fan, check out dirtyharryfilminglocations. wordpress.com for a remarkably comprehensive list of every local filming location from the 1971 film. This time, when asked, "Do you feel lucky, punk?" you can say, "Yes, because I'm in San Francisco!"

# PARADE AROUND
## THE PALACE GROUNDS IN THE MARINA

Even if you're not a member of a wedding, you can have your picture taken in the rotunda under the elegant dome at the Palace of Fine Arts at 3301 Lyon Street in the Marina. Then stroll languidly around the picturesque lagoon and exchange graceful nods with the swans on the water.

As you walk, check out the friezes of weeping women atop the Corinthian columns. Legend has it that their tears were supposed to "water" plantings in the sculpted boxes, but budget cuts and/or iffy construction nixed the needed foliage. (Now, that's something to cry about!)

Originally built for the 1915 Panama-Pacific Exposition, the Beaux-Arts-style palace is one of just a few surviving structures and the only one at the original site. It's now a designated landmark and on the National Register of Historic Places. The former exhibit hall, once used to display art from around the world, is now a 966-seat theater.

# AMUSE THE WHOLE FAMILY
## AT THE MUSÉE MÉCANIQUE

Remember Zoltar, the mechanized fortune-teller who made such a mess of Tom Hanks's young life in the movie *Big*?

Life-size puppets like that will tell your fortune at the Musée Mécanique, a quirky family-owned interactive museum where kids of all ages can examine hand-cranked musical instruments and penny arcade games from the twentieth century. For as little as a penny and as much as just fifty cents, you can also play any of the more than two hundred games and mechanized displays. (Additional machines are standing by to provide the needed change!)

A bit of San Francisco is here too, including beloved artifacts from Playland at the Beach, the Sutro Baths, and the Cliff House. Look for "Laffing Sal," "Susie the Can-Can Dancer," and "Carnival." Admission is free.

**Shed A on Pier 45**
**at the foot of Taylor Street on Fisherman's Wharf**
*415-346-2000, museemecaniquesf.com*

# SEE ART
# IN A WHOLE NEW WAY
## AT CREATIVITY EXPLORED

Creativity Explored has a truly unique mission: its sole purpose is to provide artists with developmental disabilities the means to create, exhibit, and sell their art in their studios and gallery.

The rotating exhibitions and events are truly perspective-changing, and the store—which stocks original artwork, apparel, books, and more—is a one-stop shop for some of the most original gifts you'll find. And every dollar you spend helps even more disabled people in their quest to become working artists. That's money well spent.

The gallery is open every day, and tours of the studio are available upon request.

*3245 16th Street in the Mission*
*415-863-2108, creativityexplored.org*

# COLLECT YOUR REWARD
## AT THE TOP OF OUR PUBLIC STAIRS

In a world of elevators, escalators, and people movers, the last thing some people want is to climb more stairs. Well, not San Franciscans!

This city has nearly eighty sets of public stairs scattered throughout the city. Ranging from one hundred to nearly four hundred steps, every staircase offers satisfaction along the way, whether it's peeks at local architecture, greenery, mosaic tiling, and fabulous views, or just the sense of virtue one gets with physical activity. See a side of San Francisco that many visitors don't, as you climb up and up past homes, trees, businesses, and outcroppings. It may be tough going up, but then you get to go down again.

See goo.gl/bW0Xd for a constantly updated map of San Francisco outdoor staircases, and get climbing.

# GO AVANT-GARDE
## AT ARTISTS' TELEVISION ACCESS

When San Franciscans want to drink in cutting-edge art, music, performance, and cinema, they head to Artists' Television Access, a locally based, artist-run, nonprofit organization known for fostering a supportive community for the exhibition of innovative art. The group is intensely community focused and shows an obsessive dedication to underground, nonconformist, culturally aware, and progressive exhibitions, performances, workshops, and events.

From live theater to music to the spoken word to video performance to art forms that don't even have a name yet, you can see it all at ATA, and always at a surprisingly affordable price.

Check out the calendar of events taking place while you're in town, and prepare to have your mind blown.

**Artists' Television Access**
*992 Valencia Street in the Mission*
*415-824-3890, atasite.org*

# SHOPPING AND FASHION

# INDULGE IN
# HIGH-END SHOPPING
## AT UNION SQUARE

Breakfast at Tiffany & Co., brunch at Cartier, hit Coach before lunch, stop next at Vera Wang, and then on to Jimmy Choo, the Chanel Boutique, Christian Dior, Alexander McQueen, Yves Saint Laurent, Giorgio Armani, Salvatore Ferragamo, Gucci, Hermès, Prada, and Kate Spade.

All these famous luxury shops and more are clustered on and around Union Square, an upscale shopping paradise if ever there was one.

Après shopping, take a minute to appreciate Union Square itself, a 2.6-acre plaza designed in 1847. In the center of this bustling public space is a 97-foot-tall monument to Admiral George Dewey's victory at the Battle of Manila Bay during the Spanish-American War. The name of that voluptuous statue at the top is *Victory*.

Grab a cup of coffee or an iced tea and sit for a while on one of the many benches—Union Square is a prime spot for people-watching.

**Union Square**
*Bordered by Geary, Powell, Post, and Stockton Streets downtown*
*visitunionsquaresf.com*

---

**Tip:** *Meander down nearby Maiden Lane, just off Stockton. Tiny but tony, the short street houses more boutiques and a restaurant or two. Sometimes, opera singers entertain at the end of the pedestrian mall.*

# PUT IN AT PIER 39
## ON FISHERMAN'S WHARF

Sea lion–watching is our favorite sport at Pier 39, but if you've come to shop, this is the place, with entire stores devoted to T-shirts, bath salts, cupcakes, puppets, clothing, jewelry, purses, gifts for left-handed people, sea shells, posters, seasonal decor, Irish-themed souvenirs, crystals, sports apparel, candy, and even more!

And that's just the shops.

Magicians, jugglers, musicians, and other street performers entertain here, plus the people-watching is primo. Pier 39 also boasts several restaurants (some of them legendary family-owned places), bars, cafes, and places to grab a bite of something sweet. If you are serious about your dessert, walk up the hill to the Ghirardelli Chocolate Marketplace at 900 North Point Street at Larkin and indulge in a hot fudge sundae. Remember to buy some chocolate for souvenirs.

**On the Embarcadero at Beach Street**
*415-981-7437, pier39.com*

**Tip:** *Looking for a loaf of bread shaped like a crab or a turtle?*
*Pop in at Boudin at Fisherman's Wharf, located at*
*160 Jefferson Street, just steps from Pier 39. If you have time,*
*the tour of the museum and bakery is fun.*

# SUPPORT
## SAN FRANCISCO STYLE

Finding locally made items can be tricky, but SFMade, a nonprofit organization here, makes it easier. (See sfmade.org.) They focus on developing local manufacturers that make really cool stuff that shoppers can't find anywhere else.

A lot of boutiques and small shops around town carry locally produced merchandise, and you can always ask if that's not evident. Here are three of our favorites: Gravel & Gold (clothing, cards, jewelry, and ceramics) in the Mission, Marine Layer (incredibly soft clothing for men and women) in Hayes Valley and in the Marina, and YeahYeah!PonyPrince (original, whimsical, linoleum-block-printed designs on clothing for men, women, and children) in North Beach.

Wondering where that last shop got its name? In 2009, two companies merged their businesses—and their names. We like their tees and totes and also their philosophy, a quote from E. Levy: "Human kind will begin to recover the moment we take art as seriously as physics, chemistry or money."

**Tip:** *Jillian Bornemann's cute handmade bags and totes are produced from locally sourced recycled materials. Check slaintebags.com for shops or see etsy.com/shop/slaintebags.*

# GET YOUR TIE-DYE ON
## AT THE SOCKSHOP

Whether you inhaled or you didn't, whether you remember the '60s or you don't, whether you were a genuine hippie or a clean-cut kid from the Midwest, you have to admit the wild and crazy colors and patterns of tie-dye recall all that was good about the Summer of Love in San Francisco!

Now you can bump your footwear up a notch with soft, top-quality tie-dye socks made in northern California. The family-owned Haight Street Sockshop sells them in several kaleidoscopic color combinations, and these socks are perfect inexpensive souvenirs for friends, family members, pet sitters—even your financial advisor. (Ours loves his!)

Not into tie-dye? Fine. Have it your way—this shop is sure to have novelty socks (of several lengths), leggings, and tights to tickle your fancy as well.

*1742 Haight Street in Haight-Ashbury*
*415-386-5400, sockshoponhaight.com*

**TIP:** *If you're looking for a tie-dye shirt or leggings, look at these nearby shops: Jammin' on Haight, Haight-Ashbury T-Shirts, Haight Ashbury Vintage, and the Goodwill store at Cole and Haight.*

# BOX UP
# YOUR FAVORITE PLACE
## AT CHOCOLATE COVERED

Decided on your favorite place in San Francisco?

This upscale candy store stocks hundreds of beautiful metal tins and wooden boxes that pay homage to many of our attractions. On the lid of each container is a handmade cyanotype print. (What's that? A photographic printing process that renders reverse images in white on a lovely dark blue background.)

Or maybe you've fallen in love with one of our 2,567 streets? (Remember Rod McKuen's book *Stanyan Street and Other Sorrows*?) This shop has hundreds of tins that pay tribute to the individual streets that form our complex grid. The owner prepares each box by hand, and each is coated for protection.

Wondering what to put in the box you choose? How convenient—the shop sells more than two hundred different chocolate bars and other chocolate products.

*4069 24th Street in Noe Valley*
*415-641-8123, chocolatecoveredsf.com*

**TIP:** *If you want a unique souvenir of your visit here, bring in a 4x6 print and have a custom box crafted.*

# TRY ON
# JAPANESE FASHIONS
## AT NEW PEOPLE

It's a shopping mall, it's a place to stop for a bite, it's an art gallery, it's even a destination for events—that's New People, a twenty-thousand-square-foot, five-story building that houses the best of what's new in Japanese fashion, design, and pop culture.

You can shop for clothing and accessories (at Maruk or Baby, the Stars Shine Bright), you can buy handcrafted shoes (at Sou-Sou), or you can get extensions for your eyelashes (at Lash Spot SF). Jewelry and art are also available.

Finished shopping? The New People Cinema, on the lower level, has a 143-seat theater that serves as home to several local film festivals, including the San Francisco International Film Festival, CAAMFest, Green Film Festival, and the Japan Film Festival of San Francisco. Check the schedule for what's showing next.

*1746 Post Street in Japantown*
*415-525-8630, newpeopleworld.com*

**Tip:** *Seiji Horibuchi, the owner of Viz Pictures (a Japanese film distribution company), founded New People.*

# PURCHASE AN EYE PATCH
## AT THE PIRATE SUPPLY STORE

All things pirate—glass eyes, skull-decorated dice, tri-corner pirate hats, monkey leashes, and sea salts (get it?)—are available at the Pirate Supply Store!

Beard extensions, tote bags, T-shirts, temporary tattoos, hoodies, powder horns, treasure chests, posters, flutes, spare hooks, and your basic skull bracelets are found here as well, along with any other supplies your pint-sized pirate might require. (The mysterious mermaid bait/repellant is for you.)

Jack Sparrow—excuse me, CAPTAIN Jack Sparrow—would love this place!

The Pirate Supply Store is fun and funny, but the purpose behind it is serious. Cofounded by book author Dave Eggers, the shop literally is a front for 826 Valencia, a nonprofit writing-tutoring center for students ages six to eighteen. Volunteers help young people find their voices, and all the programs are free.

*826 Valencia Street in the Mission*
*415-642-5905, ext. 201, 826valencia.org/store/*

# TREAD THE PATHS OF COMMERCE
## IN OUR NEIGHBORHOODS

Clothing boutiques, toy stores, galleries, stationery shops, and quirky specialty stores characterize the many shopping districts scattered throughout our residential neighborhoods. Coffee shops and restaurants line these same streets, so you will never go hungry while indulging in retail therapy. Here are just some of the local spots to shop:

**Fillmore Street in Lower Pacific Heights:** High-end clothing stores, interior design shops, and skin care emporiums, with some eclectic places in between. Don't miss Jonathan Adler's shop. Five blocks along Fillmore Street from Sutter Street to Clay Street.

**Hayes Valley:** A bustling neighborhood with an emphasis on antiques and home furnishings. We always pop in at Gimme Shoes, and Azalea is a great boutique. Two and a half blocks on Hayes Street between Laguna and Gough Streets.

**Chestnut Street in the Marina:** Lots of trendy clothing boutiques (including Chadwick's of London for lingerie) and a couple of major home furnishings stores. Four blocks on Chestnut Street between Divisadero and Fillmore Streets.

**Noe (pronounced No-ee) Valley:** Something for everyone in this family-friendly neighborhood. We like the Ark toy shop and also Cradle of the Sun for art glass gift items. Five blocks on 24th Street between Church and Castro Streets.

**Sacramento Street in Presidio Heights:** A posh neighborhood with high-end interior design shops, boutiques, and antique shops. Stop by Poetica Art and Antiques. Twelve blocks on Sacramento Street between Broderick and Cherry Streets.

**Union Street in Cow Hollow:** Boutiques, galleries, and jewelry shops in an area with Victorian ambiance. We like Fog City Leather, Twig, and Enchanted Crystal. Four blocks on Union Street between Fillmore and Octavia Streets.

**Valencia Street in the Mission:** Eclectic clothing shops, antique stores, and unique gift shops. Painted Bird is a favorite, as is Vanilla Saffron Imports. Four blocks between 16th and 24th Streets.

**Tip:** *Small stand-alone shops also occur elsewhere on the streets of San Francisco, and we do have two malls: the high-rise Westfield San Francisco Centre at 865 Market Street downtown and the Stonestown Galleria at 3251 20th Avenue in the Lakeside neighborhood.*

# GO BUY-BUY
## IN HAIGHT-ASHBURY

Haight-Ashbury is a legend, one with eclectic shops lining both sides of a six-block stretch from Central to Stanyan Street. Expect street musicians, homeless individuals, the occasional nearly nude person, and an overall colorful vibe.

Find custom-stained glass gifts and handcrafted jewelry at Looking Glass Collage, browse in the plethora of vintage shops, pop into Tatyana for '50s fashions, and look for crystals, candles, and statues of the popular Hindu god at the Love of Ganesha. Pipe Dreams is said to be the oldest smoke shop in the city. Tibetan clothing and souvenirs are featured in several stores. Loved to Death offers taxidermy and other uncommon gift items. And you'll find plenty of places to stop for a bite. *Note: Most stores don't open until 11 A.M.*

Don't miss the giant fishnet-clad legs sticking out the window above the Piedmont Boutique and do have your picture taken under the street signs at Haight and Ashbury.

# REFINE YOUR SURROUNDINGS
## AT THE DESIGN CENTER

Ready to rethink your decor? More than a hundred curated showrooms at the San Francisco Design Center are filled with beautiful furniture, fabrics, lighting, kitchen and bath accessories, antiques, art, rugs and flooring, cabinetry, and ceramic tile.

Three separate buildings make up the San Francisco Design Center in Showplace Square: the Showplace, the Galleria, and the Garden Court. All told, the showrooms represent more than two thousand manufacturers, some of whose product lines come from local sources and some from international sources.

You're sure to find something you like, whether you favor traditional or contemporary styles. And browsing is free!

Bargain hunters, check out the Sample Sale listings (rugs, furniture, assorted furnishings, and even closet systems) online, where you can view and purchase items directly from the SFDC showrooms.

*101 Henry Adams Street in SoMa (South of Market)*
*415-490-5800, sfdesigncenter.com*

# LET'S GET METAPHYSICAL
## AT THE SWORD & ROSE

Head down a short gangway tucked between a classy gift shop and an eclectic hair salon, pass a tiny, artful courtyard complete with fountain, and step into another world—the world of the Sword & Rose, a shop as at home in ancient times as in modern-day San Francisco.

Enter and relax in the magical ambiance. Browse the handcrafted incense, crystals, stones, and essential oils. Have a look at the jewelry, check out the books, and enjoy the unusual statuary. If you have the time, sit for a bit by the fire and cavesdrop on the fascinating conversations between customers and the shopkeepers. The longer you stay, the more items will catch your eye, so many of them delightful and unexpected at the same time. If you are in a rush, schedule a palm reading for later, just to have the perfect excuse to return to this unusual shop, which recently celebrated its twentieth anniversary.

*85 Carl Street in Cole Valley*
*415-681-5434*

# BUY RESALE
## INSTEAD OF RETAIL

Rumor has it that Julia Roberts has been sighted in San Francisco's high-end designer resale shops—so why not you? Resale of gently worn items or home furnishings is just smart recycling, and San Francisco is rabid about recycling!

**Here are just a few of the popular shops:**

**Cris**
*2056 Polk Street in the Polk Street neighborhood*
*415-474-1191, crisconsignment.com*

**Designer Consigner**
*3525 Sacramento Street in Presidio Heights*
*415-440-8664*

**Designer Consigner**
*547 Sutter Street near Union Square*
*415-362-3793*

**Goodbuys (Men's Store)**
*3464 Sacramento Street in Presidio Heights*
*415-346-6388, goodbyessf.com*

**Goodbuys (Women's Store)**
*3483 Sacramento Street in Presidio Heights*
*415-674-0151, goodbyessf.com*

## Helpers House of Couture
*(benefits the Helpers of the Mentally Retarded)*
*Nine rooms of couture fashion and jewelry*
*curated by a local philanthropist.*
*By appointment only*
*415-387-3031*

## Helpers Bazaar
*(benefit the Helpers of the Mentally Retarded)*
*900 North Point Street near Fisherman's Wharf*
*415-441-0779*

## Leftovers
*1350 Van Ness Avenue in the Polk Street neighborhood*
*415-409-0088, everybodylovesleftovers.com*

## Repeat Performance
*(benefits the San Francisco Symphony)*
*2436 Fillmore Street in Pacific Heights*
*415-563-3123*

## Seconds to Go
*(benefits Schools of the Sacred Heart)*
*2252 Fillmore Street in Pacific Heights*
*415-563-7806*

## Simply Chic
*3038 Fillmore Street in the Marina*
*415-775-2888, simplychicsf.com*

## Sui Generis Consignment—Men's
*2231 Market Street in the Castro*
*415-437-2231, suigenerisconsignment.com*

## Sui Generis Consignment—Women's
*2265 Market Street in the Castro*
*415-437-2265, suigenerisconsignment.com*

• • • • • • • • • • • • • • • • • • • • • • •

# UNCOVER YOUR MISSING PIECE
## AT A USED COOKWARE EMPORIUM

It broke, someone borrowed it and never returned it, you always liked the old one better—whatever it was, if it's no longer in your kitchen and you miss it, you'll likely find another one at Cookin', where lookin' will take some time.

In business for over thirty years, the shop is packed and stacked full of what the feisty owner calls "recycled gourmet appurtenances." Used cooking utensils, good china, better china, flatware, assorted copper pots and pans, Le Creuset, casserole dishes, Riedel wine glasses (and everyone else's too), antique egg cups, and more—it's all here. A recent trip revealed a set of six perfect port glasses, for a fraction of the original price, and our favorite cheese grater also came from Cookin'.

If the kitchen is your favorite room in your house, you'll feel right at home in these narrow aisles.

*339 Divisadero Street in the Lower Haight*
*415-861-1854*

# OPEN YOUR WALLET
## AT OUR PARKS CONSERVANCY SHOPS

Good-looking hoodies, cozy fleece jackets, and a soft scarf that pairs the colors of the Golden Gate Bridge and the fog all will keep you warm during your visit—and if you buy them from the Golden Gate National Parks Conservancy, you'll help support the system of superlative parks that enriches San Francisco.

Cool tees and sweatshirts, books, stationery, games, posters, glassware, and other splendid souvenirs are also available. Who wouldn't want a set of magnets designed to look like rivets used to build the Golden Gate Bridge? Also, the toys and books at these shops are top quality. One favorite is the set of redwood-tree stacking blocks, and we also like the kids' growth chart that features the Golden Gate Bridge.

Shop ahead of time at store.parksconservancy.org/default.asp or visit either shop when you're in town.

### Lands End Lookout Visitor Center
*680 Point Lobos Avenue in the Outer Richmond*
*415-426-5240*

### Warming Hut Cafe
*983 Marine Drive at the northwestern edge of Crissy Field*
*415-561-3042*

# BROWSE
## IN OUR MANY BOOKSTORES

Bookworms, rejoice! Many make a pilgrimage (and rightly so) to City Lights Books in North Beach, but other independent bookstores also thrive here. Most of them routinely hold readings and special events, and all offer sanctuary to readers.

### Alexander Book Company
50 Second Street in SoMa (South of Market)
415-495-2992, alexanderbook.com

### Bird & Beckett
2788 Diamond Street in Glen Park
415-586-6733, birdbeckett.com

### Books Inc.
(four locations—in the Civic Center, the Castro,
Laurel Village, and the Marina)
booksinc.net

### Bookshop
80 West Portal Avenue in West Portal
415-564 8080, bookshopwestportal.com

**Booksmith**
1644 Haight Street in Haight-Ashbury
415-863-8688, booksmith.com

**Christopher's Books**
1400 18th Street in Potrero Hill
415-255-8802, christophersbooks.com

**City Lights Books**
261 Columbus Avenue in North Beach
415-362-8193, citylights.com

**Dog Eared Books**
900 Valencia Street in the Mission
415-282-1901, dogearedbooks.com

**Green Apple Books & Music**
506 Clement Street in the Inner Richmond
415-387-2272, greenapplebooks.com

**Modern Times Bookstore**
2919 24th Street in the Mission
415-282-9246, moderntimes.com

# ATTEND A BYOB (BREAD) PARTY
## AT OLIVE THIS OLIVE THAT

Olive oil—the really good stuff—reigns supreme at this shop, and in celebration of same, the store holds a Bring Your Own Bread tasting party on the last Thursday of each month. If you miss it, just pop in any day to taste extra virgin olive oils from California and elsewhere and dark and white balsamic vinegars from Modena, Italy.

Owner Janell describes Olive This Olive That as a "boutique retailer and tasting bar," and she's always happy to talk about the benefits of and many culinary uses for olive oil. Also check out the artisan pasta, locally made sauces, hand-harvested sea salts, and body lotions made with olive oil—all great hostess gifts if you are staying with friends in San Francisco.

Need a souvenir for yourself? Pick up a beautiful handmade board, bowl, or tray made from olive wood.

*304 Vicksburg Street in Noe Valley*
*415-251-7520, olivethisolivethat.com*

**Tip:** *Find the perfect cheese (after sampling several) at Say Cheese in Cole Valley or the 24th Street Cheese Co., close to Olive This Olive That in Noe Valley.*

# SHOP
## OUR STREET VENDORS

On nice days—and most days in San Francisco are nice, what with our Mediterranean climate—wherever tourists gather you'll see clusters of booths or tables set up by licensed, local street vendors. They peddle a variety of interesting wares, including photographs, sea glass jewelry, colorful knitted caps, original paintings, tie-dyed tees, leather handbags, funky earrings and barrettes, and clothing made from natural fibers.

Look for the tables and booths in the open plaza across from the Ferry Building; some are stationed near the Hyde Street Pier, and some line downtown streets. Do follow the Law of Shopping: if you see it and you like it, buy it. The city assigns the vendors their spots on a rotating basis, and you may not be able to find your favorite a day later.

# TAKE HOME EXQUISITE TEA
## FROM LOVEJOY'S ATTIC

All things related to tea and the taking of it fill this tiny shop. In addition to a dozen or more types of loose tea, shelves here display china cups and pots, tea cozies, tea towels, and other kitchen accessories. You will also find vintage hats and gloves, perfect for your next tea party.

Once you're more than in the mood for actual tea, head across the street to Lovejoy's Tea Room and see if they can seat you for the whole enchilada—oops, for high tea, complete with delicious teensy sandwiches, scones, preserves, Devonshire cream, crumpets, and tea biscuits. (On second thought, better call 415-648-5895 ahead of time for a reservation.) And if you bought a fancy hat or you're toting your own fascinator, by all means, wear it to tea.

*1350 Church Street in Noe Valley*
*415-648-6845, lovejoystearoom.com*

# FIND AN ADORABLY CREEPY GIFT
## AT PAXTON GATE

Of course you're going to bring back gifts after you visit San Francisco! But you're way too cool to settle for the usual shot glass, "Alcatraz Swim Team" T-shirt, or cable car snow globe. Aren't you?

That's why you need to wander down to Paxton Gate to find unique treasures and oddities that meet in that strange place between the cute and the scary. Think amazing bugs, taxidermied animals, and glass eyeballs, plus jewelry and home decor also inspired by science and nature. Get a jump on Christmas shopping for your quirky teen nephew (the one who only wears black) with an articulated pigeon skeleton, or snap up some surprisingly delicate gilded antler earrings for the lady Road Warrior in your life.

If Tim Burton opened a store, this would be it!

*824 Valencia Street in the Mission*
*(The kids' store is one block up, at 766 Valencia Street.)*
*415-824-1872, paxtongate.com*

# PAMPER YOUR POOPED SELF
## AT A TOP-NOTCH SPA

Road weary? Seen too many sights? Ready to relax? San Francisco has a plethora of luxury spas waiting to soothe you with treatments not found just anywhere. Check in, chill out, and begin anew tomorrow.

**Archimedes Banya** in the Bayview combines the ancient traditions of Greek laconica, Turkish hammam, German thermen, and Russian banya (a communal bath) to promote maximum relaxation and health for the mind, body, and spirit. Cascades of warm water from seven showerheads characterize the calming Vichy shower massage, known as "Hunter's Retreat," at **Burke Williams Spa** downtown. An attendant provides additional buckets of warm water and performs gentle exfoliation. Pure bliss! A Japanese-inspired bathing facility, **Kabuki Springs & Spa** in Japantown, offers an international menu of services, including Ayurvedic massage, Thai massage, Indonesian lulur massage, Swedish massage, shiatsu, reflexology, reiki, and more.

Ahhhh—just thinking about spa treatments causes the shoulders to drop!

# SUGGESTED ITINERARIES

## OFF THE BEATEN PATH

Slurp Up a Snowy Plover at Andytown, 11
Talk to the Trees in the Botanical Garden, 50
Watch the Waves on the Pacific Ocean, 54
Contemplate the Way We Were as Seen in WPA Murals, 79
Mull the Impermanence of Man's Creations at the Sutro Baths, 80
Box Up Your Favorite Place at Chocolate Covered, 99
Try On Japanese Fashions at New People, 100
Let's Get Metaphysical at the Sword & Rose, 107
Take Home Exquisite Tea from Lovejoy's Attic, 116

## DATE NIGHT

Try a Little Tenderloin at Garibaldi's, 4
Make Like a Culture Vulture at Opera, Ballet, or Symphony, 30
Find Your New Favorite Band at NoisePop, 32
Let Your Hair Down at a Golden Gate Park Music Festival, 36
Experience Baseball San Francisco Style, 51
Rock Out on Alcatraz, 69
Raise a Glass at the California Academy of Sciences, 70
Go Avant-Garde at Artists' Television Access, 91
Pamper Your Pooped Self at a Top-Notch Spa, 118

• • • • • • • • • • • • • • • • • • • • • • • •

# ONLY IN SAN FRANCISCO

# PAMPER YOUR PALATE

# KID FRIENDLY

# FREE ACTIVITIES

• • • • • • • • • • • • • • • • • • • • • • •

# ACTIVITIES
## BY SEASON

San Francisco enjoys a moderate Mediterranean climate year-round, with temperatures ranging from about 55 at night to about 65 during the day, with rare highs of 75 to 85 on a handful of warmer days in the fall, so you can enjoy most activities here any day, any season.

## WINTER

Another Hole in the Head Genre Film Festival, 33
Bring a Bib for Dungeness Season, 23
Day of the Dead, 58
Find Your New Favorite Band at NoisePop, 32
IndieFest, 33
Lunar New Year Parade, 58
St. Patrick's Day Parade, 58

## SPRING

Asian Heritage Street Celebration, 58
Bay to Breakers, 61
Cherry Blossom Festival, 58
DocFest, 33
Escape from Alcatraz Triathlon, 61
Haight-Ashbury Street Fair, 58
North Beach Festival, 58
San Francisco Carnaval, 58

● ● ● ● ● ● ● ● ● ● ● ● ● ● ● ● ● ● ● ● ● ● ●

# SUMMER

# FALL

• • • • • • • • • • • • • • • • • • • • • •

# INDEX

• • • • • • • • • • • • • • • • • • • • • • • • • • •

● ● ● ● ● ● ● ● ● ● ● ● ● ● ● ● ● ● ● ● ● ● ● ● ● ● ●

• • • • • • • • • • • • • • • • • • • • • • •